SCHOLASTIC

GREEK MYTHOLOGY ACTIVITIES

by Marcia Worth-Baker

NEW YORK · TORONTO · LONDON · AUCKLAND · SYDNEY
MEXICO CITY · NEW DELHI · HONG KONG · BUENOS AIRES

Teaching *Resources*

DEDICATION

For David

Acknowledgments

I am grateful to the North Caldwell faculty, notably Dr. Betty Ann Wyks and Jack Venezia,
and to my many memorable AAP students. I benefited from Virginia Dooley and
Carol Ghiglieri's excellent editing. I also appreciate the encouragement of my parents,
especially my mother, Catherine Dwan. I thank David for sharing his love of the ancients,
Abby and James for their patience, and Charlie for his well-timed arrival.

Cover design by Jason Robinson

Cover illustration by Tim Jessell

Interior illustrations by Teresa Southwell except page 64 by Maxie Chambliss

Interior design by Sydney Wright

ISBN: 0-439-51788-5

Contents

Introduction

"Great are the myths." — Walt Whitman

The stories of Greek mythology are intertwined with the history of Greece, which can be traced back nearly 40,000 years. Originally passed on as oral tales, myths survived thanks to the poets Homer and Hesiod, along with historians and playwrights, who made them part of their historical and literary works. Artisans crafted pottery that told stories of the gods and goddesses. Sculptors created images of the deities, and builders designed edifices such as the Parthenon that honored particular gods and goddesses.

The myths were a part of the everyday life of ancient Greeks. Most homes boasted an altar, and daily prayer to the gods was expected. The gods' and goddesses' adventures were told and retold to instruct, explain, and entertain. Today, their stories continue to entertain us as fantastic tales, drama, and bone-chilling adventures. Gods, goddesses, heroes, and monsters have become part of our speech (see "Everyday Greek," page 58) and even our commerce (see "Mythology in the Marketplace," page 72). Greek myths have become the world's storybook, well worth reading. Although the stories are set long ago, they have much to offer readers today.

Using This Book

Activities from this book can be used sequentially or individually to teach students the structure and significance of Greek myths. Each chapter opens with a brief introduction and is followed by related activities. Teacher directions and answer keys, when needed, follow each chapter's introduction.

When you begin a unit on Greek mythology, I suggest you choose a closing activity early in the process. If you plan to do either Festival for Dionysus (page 74) or Let's Have a Pantheon! (page 73), I recommend assigning and posting students' characters early in the unit. Though students may not yet have encountered "their" character, knowing their roles will give them ownership of their god, goddess, hero, or monster. The student who plays Hades, for example, can serve as the class expert on the underworld. When a question about the underworld arises, that student can be in charge of finding the answer. Students whose research leads them to information about another student's character will enjoy sharing their findings.

Helpful classroom resources include an encyclopedia, a dictionary of classical mythology, a map of ancient Greece, and dictionaries for student use.

Memorable and Magnetic

Gods, goddesses, mortals, monsters! How do students keep them all straight? Use business-card-sized magnets (available at most office supply stores) to make—or have students make—a name plate for each character that can be posted on the board. (See the list of mythological characters on the Ask Zeus reproducible, page 34, for suggestions.) Use mailing labels or paper cut to the size of the magnets.

You can use the magnets to focus student attention on the characters who will be discussed that day, or to list the cast of characters for any myth you're studying. The magnets are a helpful visual when explaining Mount Olympus, Earth, and the underworld, and who lives where.

Many businesses whose information has changed have magnets to give away. Copy shops that produce custom-printed magnets often have overruns or "blooper" magnets to donate or sell at very low cost.

A Note on Greek Names

When the Romans conquered Greece, they adopted many of the Greeks' myths and simply renamed the characters. This book uses characters' Greek names, occasionally noting the Roman equivalent (as in Heracles' better-known Roman name, Hercules). The one exception is the Roman name Ajax, which substitutes for the harder-to-pronounce Aias. Ajax appears briefly in the Trojan War chapter.

A dictionary of classical mythology is helpful for pronunciation of Greek names, as each entry begins with a phonetic guide. As a general guideline, you may want to review the following with your students:

ae sounds like "ee," as in the word *aegis*.

c sounds like "s" when followed by *e, i, or y*. English examples include *cell, circus, cyan*.

c sounds like "k" when followed by *a, o, or u*. English examples include *cat, cot, cut*.

ch sounds like "k," as in the word *architect*.

e sounds like "ee" at the end of a name, as in the name *Penelope* or *Chloe*.

es sounds like "eez" at the end of a name, as in the name *Hercules*.

eu sounds like "yoo," as in the word *euphemism*.

oe sounds like "ee," as in *Phoebe*.

ph sounds like "f," as in *Philip*.

A Variety of Accounts

Because the myths were passed along orally, differing versions were in circulation. For some mythological stories two, three, or more variations exist, and no particular account is definitive. Because of this, as you and your students investigate these myths, you may find alternate versions from the ones offered here.

CHAPTER 1

Getting Started With Myths

Myths are concerned with fundamental issues that are as meaningful today as they were thousands of years ago. How should we behave? Why are things the way they are? These are questions all of us ask, and which the myths were fashioned to answer.

The activities that follow make for good openers to your mythology unit. Here you can give students an introduction to what myths are, and give them an opportunity to try their hand at crafting a myth of their own.

What Is a Myth?

A good way to introduce mythology is to read a myth together as a class. The story of Demeter and Persephone is a well-known myth, and it introduces students to one of the key themes of Greek mythology: for good or ill, the actions of immortals have an impact on mortals.

Demeter

MATERIALS

§ What Is a Myth reproducible, pages 9–10

HERE'S HOW

1. Pass out copies of the What Is a Myth? reproducible. Using the pronunciation tips on page 5 or a dictionary of classical mythology, review the Greek names that appear in the story.

2. Read "The Seasons of the Year" (page 9) aloud or silently. Answer the questions that follow the excerpt as a class or individually.

3. Lead students in a discussion of the myth. Are they satisfied with this explanation of why the earth has seasons? Why or why not?

Answers: 1. The four seasons of the year. 2. Answers will vary, but may include: immortals argue, immortals feel sadness, immortals ask one another for help. 3. Answers will vary, but may include: Demeter has the ability to make things grow. Zeus commands the other gods to do his bidding. Hades lives in the underworld. All the gods and goddesses can travel throughout the world. 4. Answers will vary.

Writing a Myth

At any point in your study of Greek mythology, you may want to have your students write their own myths. The sheet on page 11 guides students through myth prewriting, and introduces the literary terms *protagonist*, *antagonist*, and *setting*. Although the directions below refer to writing a class myth, the worksheet can also be used for individual writing projects. Myths in the Night Sky, the reproducible that follows, contains a specific myth-based writing assignment.

MATERIALS

- Writing a Myth reproducible (page 11)

HERE'S HOW

1. Many myths offer creative explanations for natural occurrences. Explain to students that together they will write a myth that explains the origin or cause of a natural event. The myth will include a description of the event, a protagonist, an antagonist, their conflict, and a setting. The natural event will result from the actions of the protagonist and the antagonist in the setting.

2. As a class, take a walk or observe nature from the classroom windows. Ask students to list natural events or phenomena that they see. Together choose one to explain through your myth.

3. Ask the class to brainstorm a hero for their story. This will be the protagonist.

4. Ask the class to brainstorm an opponent for their hero. This will be the antagonist.

5. Lead the class in choosing a time and place for their story that makes sense for their characters and their natural event. For example, the sky is an appropriate setting for a myth explaining the origin of the clouds.

6. Ask the class to imagine a conflict that might arise between their characters in their chosen setting. For example, in the sky, thunder and lightning might vie to see which is more powerful. The result of this conflict will be the natural event that the class has chosen to explain.

7. When the class is satisfied with their choices, lead students in writing a group draft, or individual rough drafts.

8. After editing and proofreading, complete a final draft to read aloud or act out. Include an exciting title!

Myths in the Night Sky

Many familiar constellations were identified by the ancient Greeks and named for mythological characters and places. Orion the Hunter is one of the easier constellations to find in the night sky. If students won't have the opportunity to see for themselves, they can visit the National Geographic Web site (**http://www.nationalgeographic.com/features/97/stars/chart/index.html**), which features many Hubble Space Telescope images of the constellation Orion.

MATERIALS

💰 Myths in the Night Sky reproducible (page 12)

HERE'S HOW

1. Pass out copies of the reproducible. Ask a student to read aloud the introduction and the myth.

2. Direct students to look for Orion in the night sky or, if conditions don't permit, at the National Geographic Web site. The following day, discuss what they saw in this group of stars.

3. Have students complete the activity following the myth.

Answers: Answers will vary.

The Geography of Ancient Greece

Listed below are a number of Internet sites that feature maps of ancient Greece. For comparison, your students might want to view a map of the ancient world and then a map of modern Europe. Maps of modern Greece and other European countries can be found at **http://www.viamichelin.com/viamichelin/gbr/dyn/controller/Maps**.

To illustrate how Greeks used mythology to explain the natural world, read aloud the following description of the ancient world and ask students to sketch it. When they are finished, compare what they drew to a map of the terrain, such as that found at **www.unc.edu/awmc/awmcmap16.html**. (Choose Version 4 for terrain only.)

At the center of the known world was Earth, a land of mountains, coastlines, and islands. Surrounding Earth was a stretch of water called Ocean, which was controlled by Poseidon. At the end of the known world, the River Styx flowed out of the Ocean and formed a barrier to the underworld. To cross into the underworld, dead souls had to pay the ferryman, Charon, one coin. Above Earth was Mount Olympus, where the most important of the gods and goddesses lived.

Maps of the Ancient World

Interactive ancient Mediterranean
http://iam.classics.unc.edu/map/map_idx.html

Map of Greece and Asia Minor
http://www2.roanoke.edu/religion/maclean/Heroikos/MapG&AM.html

Map of Aegean Sea and Greece:
http://www.unc.edu/awmc/awmcmap16.html

What Is a Myth?

To the ancient Greeks, myths were both education and entertainment. Some myths explained natural events, and others taught mortals about the ways of the gods. Although the ancient Greeks believed that the gods and goddesses looked and acted a lot like them, they also believed the immortals had special powers, which the myths served to illustrate. Most myths also reminded mortals how the gods preferred to be treated—with honor and respect!

Today we still know about these myths because they were eventually written down by playwrights and poets. But for centuries the myths were simply oral tales, passed by word of mouth from storyteller to listener.

The following is a well-known Greek myth. Read it and answer the questions that follow.

The Seasons of the Year

Happy Demeter, goddess of the harvest, made the world's plants and trees bloom and grow all year. Her daughter, Persephone, helped her in this work. All was well when they were together, and Demeter allowed the mortals to enjoy the fruits and vegetables that she grew on Earth.

Zeus' brother Hades, god of the underworld, loved Persephone from afar. He asked Zeus, who was not only the king of the gods but also Persephone's father, for permission to marry her. Zeus didn't say yes, because he knew Demeter would never part with her daughter. But he also didn't say no, as he was loyal to his brother. Finally, Hades decided to act for himself.

One day, when Persephone was alone in a meadow, Hades kidnapped her and took her to the underworld. In that dark place, where almost nothing grew, Persephone was miserable. She refused to drink or eat anything except a few pomegranate seeds.

Demeter was equally miserable without her daughter, and she neglected the world's plants as she searched for Persephone. Harvests failed, trees and plants withered. The mortals were in danger of starving.

When Demeter finally discovered Persephone in the underworld, she begged Zeus for help.

"Command Hades to release our daughter!" she cried. "Look at her! Persephone is withering away like the plants of the earth."

Zeus agreed. "As long as Persephone hasn't eaten any food of the dead she shall be free."

"I ate almost nothing," cried Persephone from inside the underworld's gates. "Just six pomegranate seeds."

What Is a Myth? (Continued)

"Then you shall spend six months of each year as Queen of the underworld," said Zeus. "The other six months you may live with your mother."

Though Demeter and Persephone cried and pleaded, Zeus was firm. For six months every year, Persephone stayed with Hades in the underworld. While Demeter mourned for her daughter, Earth's plants and trees drooped, withered, and died. When Persephone returned and Demeter rejoiced, the growing things revived and bloomed again.

QUESTIONS

1. What natural event does this myth explain?

_____

_____

_____

2. In what ways do the immortals in this story act like humans?

_____

_____

_____

3. What abilities do the immortals in this story have that humans lack?

_____

_____

_____

4. As an ancient Greek hearing this story for the first time, what lessons might you learn about the gods and goddesses?

_____

_____

_____

_____

Writing a Myth

A good way to begin writing a myth is to recall a natural event that you have witnessed. Some examples include the seasonal migration of birds, the changing color of the leaves, and thunder and lightning. Choose one of these, or select one of your own, and write a myth to describe its origins.

What is the natural event that you are going to explain in your myth?

Choose a hero for your story. The literary term for this character is *protagonist*. Name and describe your *protagonist*.

Choose a character with whom your character will argue or battle. The literary term for this character is *antagonist*. Name and describe your *antagonist*.

Describe the time and place in which your characters live. This is the *setting* of your myth.

Imagine a conflict that might arise between these characters. The result of this conflict will be the natural event that you described at the top of the page.

When you have completed this page, begin your rough draft on a separate sheet of paper. After editing and proofreading your draft, complete a final revision to share with your classmates. Give your myth an exciting title.

Myths in the Night Sky

What do you see when you look into the night sky? The stargazers of ancient Greece saw constellations, groups of stars that appeared to bear the shapes of mythological creatures and characters. Many of the names they gave to the stars are names we still use today. We know now that the constellation Orion the Hunter is a group of stars located 1,500 light-years away, along a spiral arm of the Milky Way. To the ancient Greeks, however, it was the mighty hunter Orion himself, who was punished for his misdeeds.

Read the myth of Orion and follow the directions below.

The Myth of Orion

Poseidon, god of the sea, had a son named Orion, who was gifted with great skill as a hunter but cursed with poor judgment. Eos, goddess of the dawn, fell in love with him, but Orion was not true to her. He chose to go hunting with Artemis, the goddess of hunting and the moon. Orion boasted to Artemis that he was such a skilled hunter that he could kill all of the world's wild beasts and monsters. Artemis' brother Apollo did not trust Orion and did not consider him a good match for his sister. When he heard of Orion's boastful claim, he asked Mother Earth to send a huge scorpion to attack Orion. Orion fought valiantly, but he realized that his mortal skills were no match for the scorpion. Hoping for Eos's protection, Orion plunged into the ocean and swam toward the island of Delos to reach her.

As he swam toward the island, though, Eos wasn't waiting for him, but Artemis was. Apollo joined her there. As he and Artemis stood on the shore, he saw a tiny figure far off in the distance and recognized that it was Orion, swimming toward the island. Apollo challenged his sister to hit the small, distant shape in the ocean with her arrow. Artemis shot accurately and killed Orion.

When Artemis realized what she had done, she pleaded with Asclepius, the god of healing, to restore Orion to life. Zeus, King of the gods, forbade Asclepius to do so, so Artemis placed Orion's image in the sky, where the scorpion, the constellation Scorpio, still chases him among the stars.

Choose a group of stars visible to you in the night sky and sketch them on another piece of paper. What shape do see in the stars? Create a myth to explain how your stars reached the sky.

CHAPTER 2

Mighty Mount Olympus!

Zeus

The mythical Mount Olympus, where the most important of the ancient Greek gods and goddesses lived, probably took its name from the real Mount Olympus, located in central Greece. But the mythical Mount Olympus was located somewhere above the earth, and its residents traveled freely between realms. Some visited the underworld. And, according to Homer, some gods and goddesses vacationed in Ethiopia.

The ancient Greeks created for themselves a legion of mighty gods and goddesses who could travel instantly, change shapes, and even inspire war and love. Male and female gods and goddesses often had equivalent powers. At the same time, ancient Greeks gave their gods human failings, such as jealousy and infidelity. This resulted in complex familial relationships, with half-mortal men and women roaming the earth while their immortal parent's aunts, uncles, and cousins watched from Mount Olympus.

There are four main classes of gods. The Olympians make up the first group, and they are the focus of this chapter. The second class consists of the gods and goddesses who lived elsewhere (you'll encounter many of them in the activity Zeus Says: A Game of the Gods, page 18). The third group is made up of demi-gods and heroes. Demi-gods are the children of a mortal and an immortal. Heroes, such as Heracles (see chapter 3), are the very few mortals whose heroic deeds raised them to the rank of the gods. The fourth group includes the personifications of virtues and vices, such as fear, patience, and envy. While countless temples were raised by ancient Greeks to honor their gods and goddesses, the great majority honor Apollo, Athena, Poseidon, and Zeus.

This chapter will introduce students to the Olympian gods and goddesses through myths, games, and classroom activities.

*T*he Beginning of the World

This ancient Greek myth explains how the physical world was formed and filled with gods and goddesses. The activity that follows introduces students to ancient Greek names that have become part of our modern vocabulary.

MATERIALS

§ The Beginning of the World reproducible (pages 20–21)   § dictionaries

HERE'S HOW

1. Read (either as a class or individually) "Chaos, Titans, and the New Gods at Battle."

2. Direct students to the chart that follows the story. Have students fill in the words' meanings as they are used in the story.

3. Ask students to fill in the modern meanings of the words using their own knowledge or a dictionary.

Extension: Direct students, as a class or individually, to begin keeping a list of myth-based words that they discover throughout the unit.

Answers: Atlas: a giant who held up Earth; a book containing maps. Chaos: a state of nothingness; a state of disorganization and confusion. Olympian/Olympus: the mountain where some of the gods lived; superior, great. Titanic/Titan: A race of giants; very large. Panic/Pan: a goat god; extreme worry or nervousness.

*H*ow Mortals Were Made

This activity introduces students to the ancient Greeks' creation myth. It also demonstrates that stories told orally change in the retelling.

MATERIALS

§ drawing paper   § crayons, markers, or colored pencils

HERE'S HOW

1. Remind students that for a very long time, the myths were transmitted orally and weren't written down. That's why there are so many variations to some of the stories. Each time the tale was told, certain elements were altered.

2. Read "How Mortals Were Made" (page 15) to the class. Tell students that after you read it to them, they are going to retell it to each other.

3. After pairs or small groups have shared the story with one another, ask them to illustrate a scene. Ask students if drawing a picture of a story helps them to remember it better.

How Mortals Were Made

Long, long ago, the Golden Race of men appeared on Earth. Because there were no women, the Golden Race died out, and Zeus replaced them with the Silver Race. These men and women fought often and ignored the gods, so Zeus sent them to the underworld.

Now, Prometheus, a Titan, tried to create people to live on Earth. He decided to make people who resembled gods so mortals and immortals could better understand each other. The people he made were called the Bronze Race.

Prometheus often tried to help the mortals he had created. When he saw them shivering in the cold and eating raw meat, he decided to give them fire.

With Athena's help, Prometheus stole fire from Zeus' palace and taught the mortals how to use it. Suddenly, people could cook, keep warm, and even forge metal tools.

Zeus was angry at what Prometheus had done, and he punished the mortals, sending a nine-day flood to drown them all. However, Deucalion and his wife, Pyrrha, survived and thanked Zeus for his protection.

When he saw this, Zeus was pleased that two humans had survived. He sent the Titaness, Themis, to Earth. "Follow me," she instructed the humans, "and drop rocks behind you as you walk."

Where Deucalion dropped rocks, men appeared. Where Pyrrha dropped rocks, women appeared. Earth again filled with humans. These were the people of the Age of Heroes, which lasted until the Trojan War.

Welcome to Mount Olympus!

There are countless Greek gods and goddesses, but those who lived on Mount Olympus appear most often in myths and were probably the most familiar to the ancient Greeks. Officially there were 12 Olympians, although Hades and Hestia are counted here, for a total of 14. Hades left Mount Olympus to reside in the underworld. And Hestia gave up her throne to guard the palace hearth. As they do this activity, students will discover that in the minds of the ancient Greeks, each of the Olympians had a personality, a responsibility, and a family, and was associated with particular symbols. Students may also discover factual inconsistencies from one source to another if they research the gods and goddesses—proof, again, that oral tales change in the telling.

MATERIALS

- gods and goddesses fact sheets (pages 22–28)
- sheets of 8 1/2 - by-11-inch paper
- markers
- glue
- stapler
- ruler

HERE'S HOW

1. Distribute copies of the gods and goddesses fact sheets. To familiarize students with the gods and goddesses, read aloud the description of each. Students can then cut and staple the sheets to make a reference book of their own. This booklet will be a handy resource throughout their study of Greek mythology.

2. To make the booklets, students cut the fact sheets along the dashed lines to create fourteen pages. They then staple the left edges together. If desired, have them create a cover for the book using construction paper. Let them decorate their books, if they like.

Ask-a-God

Ancient Greeks directed their requests and their thanks to specific gods and goddesses. This activity will help students become more familiar with the particular interests of the Olympian gods and goddesses.

MATERIALS

֍ Ask-a-God reproducible (page 29)

֍ God and goddess fact sheets (pages 22–28), or booklet made in previous activity

HERE'S HOW

1. Distribute the reproducible and ask a student to read aloud the directions.

2. Direct students to refer to their god and goddess fact sheets or booklets in order to complete the activity. You may wish to have students work in pairs.

Extension: Students can write their own "Ask-a-God" questions to gods and goddesses who don't appear in this activity. Have them exchange questions with classmates.

Answers: 1. Demeter, goddess of agriculture and harvests 2. Artemis, goddess of hunting 3. Apollo, sun god and god of healing 4. Aphrodite, goddess of love 5. Poseidon, god of the sea

It's Fate

This game introduces students to the ancient Greeks' beliefs about fate and what happened to mortals after death. The Fate cards introduce students to some famous instances of reward and punishment from the gods.

MATERIALS

(for each pair of students)

֍ game board (pages 30–31)

֍ a set of Fate cards (page 32), cut out and stacked facedown

֍ one die

֍ two game markers (coins, buttons, paper clips, etc.)

֍ scrap paper, pencil, dictionary

HERE'S HOW

1. Read aloud the description below, to introduce your students to the Greek ideas about fate and the afterlife. (For younger students, you may wish to summarize.) If you prefer to play the game without discussing fate and the afterlife, simply explain that each player's objective is to reach the board's center.

The ancient Greeks believed that their lives were dictated by the gods and goddesses. Both in the earthly life and after death, the Greeks believed that those who displeased the gods were punished and those who pleased the gods were greatly rewarded.

The Greeks believed that all mortals went to the underworld after death, although they thought many were eventually sent back to Earth to live another life. To get to the underworld they paid the ferryman Charon to cross the River Styx. Once having crossed the river, a mortal might go to one of three places:

__Tartarus__ was the region of the underworld reserved for those who did evil deeds on Earth.

__Asphodel Fields__, where most people went, was like Earth, but people were shadowy versions of their Earthly selves.

__Elysian Fields__ was a beautiful and happy place. People whose lives had pleased the gods were allowed to go here.

2. Distribute a game board and a set of Fate cards to each pair of students. Read aloud the game's rules and objectives below, and allow students time to play the game at least once.

> On a desk or table, arrange a game board, a set of Fate cards, cut apart and stacked facedown, two game markers, a dictionary, and scrap paper.

> With your partner, take turns rolling the die. The player who rolls the lower number goes first.

> Starting on Earth, take turns rolling the die and moving your marker the appropriate number of spaces along the board.

> When you land on a space, follow the directions printed in that space. When you land on a FATE space, pick up a card and follow the instructions. Place discarded FATE cards at the bottom of the card pile.

> The winning player is the one who reaches the Elysian Fields first.

NOTE: If you wish to have students play more than one time, they may play until one player has reached the Elysian Fields three times. Some ancient Greeks believed that a mortal who did so went to the Blessed Isles for eternity.

Oracles and Omens

The ancient Greeks consulted the gods before making big decisions, but they didn't receive advice directly. Sometimes the gods were believed to speak through soothsayers, people who claimed to see into the future. The most famous soothsayer in Greek mythology was the Trojan princess Cassandra. It was

said that she was cursed by Apollo with both the power to predict the future and the inability to convince anyone of the truth of what she saw.

Some Greeks sought advice from an *oracle*. An oracle was a priestess who purportedly spoke for a god. (The term *oracle* can also refer to the place where this speaking was done, or the message itself.) The most famous oracle was the sibyl at Delphi—a priestess named Pythia. It was said that Apollo spoke through her. Many Greek leaders traveled to Delphi before making decisions of state.

Ordinary Greeks also consulted priests who were trained to interpret signs, or *omens*, such as the behavior of animals, weather, and even the patterns made by animal entrails. These priests helped the ancient Greeks understand what behavior the gods would reward or punish, and counseled them about how to act in the future.

MATERIALS

🖐 Oracles and Omens reproducible (page 33)

HERE'S HOW

1. Read aloud or summarize for your students the information above on oracles and omens.

2. Distribute the reproducible and explain to students that they will imagine they are Nestor, a wise old man who understood the ways of the immortals. Have students use their knowledge of the gods and goddesses, as well as their own imagination, to interpret events that trouble their neighbors. If you like, do the first one together. The class can brainstorm an answer, or you can read the sample answer below.

3. Direct students to complete the activity individually, or orally in pairs.

Answers: 1. (sample answer) Zeus is angry that you turned away a stranger who came to your door. If you give the next beggar you see the finest sheep in your flock, Zeus will forgive you. Your husband will again catch many fish. Other answers will vary.

Zeus Says: A Game of the Gods

When the ancient Greeks spoke to the gods, they stood in one of four positions. The Greeks believed that the gods had strong preferences about how they preferred to be addressed.

Zeus Says helps students become familiar with the Olympians and aware of some of the lesser gods and goddesses.

MATERIALS

🖐 Zeus Says reproducible (page 34)

HERE'S HOW

1. Distribute the reproducible. Initially, you may wish to play the game with an abbreviated list. You can add more gods and goddesses as your students encounter them.

2. Read aloud the names of the gods and goddesses once for familiarity.

3. With the class, practice the four positions described and modeled on page 34.

4. Ask one student to take the part of Zeus, or caller. That student will call the names of gods and goddesses at random while the class takes the appropriate position. Students can take turns "being" Zeus until the end of the allotted time; or play elimination-style.

Extensions: Ask students if any of the gods' names sound like modern words. List and define them.

Have students look up information on the "lesser" gods named in this activity. Divide the class into three groups—Marine, Sky, and Underworld—and have each group gather information about the gods and goddesses in their domain. Ask the groups to share what they've learned.

*C*ount on Athena!

The ancient Greeks believed that Athena, goddess of wisdom and war, invented numbers. She shared her knowledge only with men, but some women did learn to read and write numbers.

MATERIALS

⚬ Count on Athena! reproducible (pages 35–36)

HERE'S HOW

1. Distribute the activity sheets and ask students to read the introduction and directions.

2. Direct students to complete the number problems.

NOTE: You may want to post or reproduce the number chart on an overhead projector.

Extension: Ask students to create a large number line to post in the classroom.

Answers:

1. 87	2. 545	3. 884
4. ΥΚΑ	5. ΞΔ	6. ΩΝΘ
7. ΙΔ	8. Δ	9. Η
10. 78 − 33 = 45 (ΜΕ)	11. 837 − 452 = 385 (ΤΠΕ)	
12. 70 × 4 = 280 (ΣΠ)	13. 280/14 = 20 (Κ)	
14. 749/7 = 107 (ΡΖ)	15. Answers will vary.	

The Beginning of the World

The story the ancient Greeks told about the beginning of the world explains how the universe was divided into four parts: Earth, the underworld, the sea, and the sky, where Mount Olympus is located. Although Mount Olympus is a real mountain in Greece, the name came to mean an imaginary place where many of the Greek gods were believed to live. Likewise, you will find words in the following story whose modern meaning and form have changed from what they originally were to the ancient Greeks.

Read "Chaos, Titans, and the New Gods at Battle." At the end of the story, complete the chart that follows. You may want to consult a dictionary for help.

Chaos, Titans, and the New Gods at Battle

The world began in a state of nothingness called Chaos. Slowly, Mother Earth emerged from Chaos and produced a generation of giants called Titans. Cronos, the king of these Titans, married Rhea, and they had five children. But Cronos was so jealous and power hungry that he swallowed them all. When Rhea had her last child, Zeus, she tricked Cronos into swallowing a stone instead, so that the child would live.

As Zeus grew up, he plotted revenge against his father for swallowing his brothers and sisters. He knew that, because they were immortal, his brothers and sisters had not died when they were swallowed. They were still inside Cronos, waiting to be rescued. One day, Zeus slipped a bitter potion into Cronos' drink. When Cronos choked, Hestia, Demeter, Hera, Hades, and Poseidon came tumbling out of him.

A fierce battle between the Titans and Cronos' children followed. Zeus hurled huge boulders down the side of Mount Olympus. Pan, the young goat god, shouted that the world was ending. The Titans feared the mountain's collapse and fled. The younger gods, called the New Gods, won control of Earth. Zeus banished the Titans, except for Atlas, who was sentenced to hold up Earth forever.

The three brothers, Zeus, Poseidon, and Hades, divided the world. Zeus took control of the sky and Mount Olympus, Hades became god of the underworld, and Poseidon controlled the sea. Zeus' three sisters, Hestia, Demeter, and Hera, joined him on Mount Olympus.

The Beginning of the World (Continued)

Fill in the chart with each word's meaning in the story and in modern usage. You will notice that some of the words have changed slightly, so the original form is in parentheses.

	Meaning in the story	Modern meaning
Atlas		
Chaos		
Olympian (Olympus)		
Titanic (Titan)		
Panic (Pan)		

APHRODITE

Occupation: Goddess of love and beauty

Responsibilities: Helping mortals and immortals to fall in love

Powers: Causing mortals and immortals to fall in love

Symbols: Rose, dove, sparrow, dolphin, ram, apple, myrtle

Weapons: A magic girdle that inspired love

Home: Mount Olympus

Parents: Zeus and Dione

Married to: Hephaestus

Hobbies: Flirting

Interesting Information: Aphrodite was born in the sea and rode to shore on a shell. She is usually pictured with a mirror.

APOLLO

Occupation: Sun god; god of medicine, music, poetry, dance, math, herdsmen, and prophecy

Responsibilities: Controlling the sun's daily movement across the sky

Powers: Healing, inspiring learning, making the sun rise and set

Symbols: Laurel tree, lyre, the number 7

Weapons: Bow and arrow

Home: Mount Olympus

Parents: Zeus and Leto

Married to: Unmarried

Hobbies: Known for killing many mythological monsters

Interesting Information: Apollo is Artemis' twin.

ARES

Occupation: God of war

Responsibilities: Waging war

Powers: Inciting conflict

Symbols: Dog, vulture, spear, flaming torch

Weapons: Spear

Home: Mount Olympus

Parents: Zeus and Hera

Married to: Unmarried

Hobbies: Violence

Interesting Information: Among the other gods and goddesses, only Hades, Aphrodite, and Eros would speak to Ares. He was disliked for his violent temper.

ARTEMIS

Occupation: Goddess of the moon and hunting

Responsibilities: Protecting women, animals, and cities

Powers: Changing people into animals

Symbols: Cypress tree, dog, deer, bird

Weapons: Silver bow and arrow

Home: Mount Olympus

Parents: Zeus and Leto

Married to: Unmarried

Hobbies: Punishing hunters who killed more game than they needed to eat

Interesting Information: Apollo's twin, Artemis was known to be very independent.

ATHENA

Occupation: Goddess of wisdom and war

Responsibilities: Giving wisdom, inspiring inventions, protecting Athens

Powers: Changing herself into other shapes and forms

Symbols: Owl, olive tree

Weapons: Lance, shield, fringed cloak

Home: Mount Olympus

Parents: Zeus and Metis, a Titaness

Married to: Unmarried

Hobbies: Patron goddess of Athens; invented math

Interesting Information: Athena accidentally shot her childhood friend Pallas with a bow and arrow, so she is sometimes called Pallas Athena.

DEMETER

Occupation: Goddess of agriculture, guardian of marriage

Responsibilities: Controlling the harvest

Powers: Able to make plants and trees grow or die

Symbols: Torch, sheaf of wheat or barley

Weapons: None

Home: Mount Olympus

Parents: Cronos and Rhea

Married to: Unmarried

Hobbies: Disguised as an old woman, Demeter roamed the earth rewarding some cities with good harvests and punishing others with poor harvests.

Interesting Information: Demeter created the four seasons.

DIONYSUS

Occupation: God of wine and parties

Responsibilities: Cupbearer to the gods

Powers: Creating happiness or unhappiness for mortals

Symbols: Grape vine, ivy wreath, rose, drinking vessel (cup)

Weapons: None

Home: Mount Olympus

Parents: Zeus and Semele, a mortal

Married to: Unmarried

Hobbies: Attending parties; teaching mortals how to grow grapes and make wine

Interesting Information: Dionysus became associated with drama. He is the youngest of the Olympian gods.

HADES

Occupation: God of the dead

Responsibilities: Ruling the underworld; guarding the dead

Powers: Causing death

Symbols: Cornucopia

Weapons: cap of invisibility

Home: The underworld

Parents: Cronos and Rhea

Married to: Persephone

Hobbies: Riding in a gold chariot drawn by black horses

Interesting Information: He is Zeus' brother. The underworld is sometimes called Hades. Hades himself was very wealthy, as he owned all the precious stones and metals found in the earth.

HEPHAESTUS

Occupation: God of blacksmiths, craftsmen, and fire

Responsibilities: Granting power to blacksmiths; helping mortals to create useful items

Powers: Able to create objects with magical properties

Symbols: Axe, tongs

Weapons: Blacksmith tongs, hammer

Home: Mount Olympus, but his forge is in the crater of Mount Aetna, a volcano in Sicily

Parents: Zeus and Hera

Married to: Aphrodite

Hobbies: Famous creations include Achilles' weapons, Odysseus' weapons, Heracles' shield, Agamemnon's scepter, and Harmonia's necklace

Interesting Information: Because he was born ugly, his mother threw him from Mount Olympus. He lived in the sea for nine years.

HERA

Occupation: Queen of the gods; goddess of women and motherhood

Responsibilities: Watching over women

Powers: Commanding the winds

Symbols: Peacock, pomegranate

Weapons: Trickery, deceit

Home: Mount Olympus

Parents: Cronos and Rhea

Married to: Zeus

Hobbies: Punishing the goddesses and mortal women that Zeus pursued, punishing their children, ordering other gods to help her inflict her punishments

Interesting Information: Hera spends much of her time chasing after Zeus, his lovers, and their children. Thus, she travels frequently throughout the world.

HERMES

Occupation: Messenger of the gods; god of dreams, commerce, treaties, inventions, science, art, and oratory

Responsibilities: Patron of voyagers and thieves; delivers the gods' messages; escorts the dead to the underworld

Powers: Traveling anywhere instantly

Symbols: The number 4, a staff with wings, the caduceus

Weapons: None; Hermes' staff bore a white ribbon,

which marked his neutrality in any conflict.

Home: Mount Olympus

Parents: Zeus and Maia, a Titaness

Married to: Unmarried

Hobbies: Creating mischief; As an infant, Hermes stole Apollo's cattle but Apollo forgave him when Hermes invented the lyre for him.

Interesting Information: "Hermes" means hastener.

HESTIA

Occupation: Goddess of the hearth and marriage

Responsibilities: Protector of orphans and the home

Powers: None, although she held great influence with the other gods and goddesses

Symbols: None, but almost every home had a shrine to her

Weapons: None

Home: Mount Olympus

Parents: Cronos and Rhea

Married to: Unmarried

Hobbies: Protecting homes

Interesting Information: As the most sacred of the Olympians, Hestia was considered too good for gossip. She eventually gave up her throne to Dionysus to tend the palace hearth.

POSEIDON

Occupation: God of the sea

Responsibilities: Overseeing the oceans and navigation

Powers: Causing and quelling earthquakes, storms; rousing sea monsters

Symbols: Horse, dolphin, pine tree

Weapons: The trident, a three-pronged spear

Home: Mount Olympus and all bodies of water

Parents: Cronos and Rhea

Married to: Amphitrite

Hobbies: Riding a gold chariot with white horses

Interesting Information: He was Zeus' brother. He invented the horse and the dolphin.

ZEUS

Occupation: King of the gods

Responsibilities: Ruler of Mount Olympus, Earth, and sky; ruler of all mortals and immortals

Powers: Can change himself into any form; can banish others to the underworld or bestow immortality

Symbols: Eagle, oak tree

Weapons: Thunderbolts, lightning

Home: Mount Olympus

Parents: Cronos and Rhea

Married to: Hera

Hobbies: Courting goddesses and mortal women; hiding from Hera; administering justice among mortals and immortals

Interesting Information: Zeus led the new gods, many of whom were his siblings, to victory over the Titans. He built the palace on Mount Olympus.

Ask-a-God

The ancient Greeks directed their prayers and requests for help to the gods and goddesses whose special abilities addressed their problems.

Using your god and goddess booklet, decide which god or goddess each of the ancient Greeks below might ask for help. Write the name and "occupation" on the line.

1. Dear _____,

    I sowed many acres of grain and carefully tended the fields. With your help I will yield a good harvest. Will you grant me a plentiful crop that will feed me and my family through the winter?

Nikos the Farmer

2. Dear _____,

    Our fair city of Lailos will soon begin our annual boar hunt. We have always been loyal to you, goddess, and we will hunt only as much as we need to sustain our people. Can you grant us successful hunting?

The Citizens of Lailos

3. Dear_____,

    Oh powerful god, can you please help my most prized ram, who was badly stung by bees last night? He is badly hurt. Turn your healing power, like the glorious rays of the sun, to my humble flock of sheep.

Kalos the Shepherd

4. Dear _____,

    I long to fall in love! Goddess, please send a brave, true man to my little village. Cause him to fall in love with me, so we can be married by spring.

Atla the Lovelorn

5. Dear _____,

    I have long been your loyal servant. In return, can you protect me and my crew as we sail the seas to Lemnos? Grant us calm waters and high tides.

Senna the Sailor

FATE

List three of Zeus' good qualities to advance three spaces.

Poseidon is angry. A tidal wave sends you back two spaces.

Hermes asks you to help him deliver a message to Mount Olympus. Will you risk it! If yes, take a FATE card. If no, miss a turn.

Help Hestia tend the hearth. Stay here until your next turn.

FATE

Hephaestus makes you a marvelous suit of armor. Thank him and move ahead two spaces.

You forgot to thank Demeter for a good harvest. Move back one space.

Atlas asks you to hold Earth for him. Agree and lose a turn or risk moving ahead to the nearest FATE space.

Tell Hera where Zeus is hiding. She'll reward you by advancing you one space.

Happy Hunting! Thank Artemis for the successful hunts so she will advance you two spaces.

S·T·A·R·T

IT'S FATE

FATE

You saw
Athena bathing
and she turned
you into a statue.
Move back
two spaces.

Ares sends
you into battle.
Miss one turn.

Aphrodite smiles
upon you.
Advance to the
River Styx.

You had a successful
day selling your
crops in the agora
(marketplace). Rest here
until your next turn.

FATE

Apollo is
angry today.
He doesn't let the sun
rise, and sends you
back to Earth.

Place
FATE
cards here.

You are almost
at the River Styx.
Pay Charon
the boatman
one obol (coin)
to row you across.
Give up one turn.

It's the Festival of
Dionysus! Stay at the
party (on this space)
until your next turn.

The River Styx

FATE

Hades wants you
to visit him in the
underworld.
Miss one turn
while you're away.

Welcome to
the Elysian
Fields!
Enjoy your
stay!

F·I·N·I·S·H

Echo, a nymph, kept Hera busy while Zeus chased other nymphs. To punish her, Hera said, "You can never speak your thoughts again. You can only repeat the last words others say." *Say nothing until your next turn!*

Narcissus was punished by Artemis. She caused him to fall in love with his own reflection in a pool of water. In despair, he stabbed himself. His drops of blood became the flower called narcissus. *Draw a flower.*

When Psyche's parents boasted that, "Our daughter is as beautiful as Aphrodite," Aphrodite punished Psyche. Zeus intervened and made Psyche immortal. *Imagine you are Psyche and thank Zeus.*

Tantalus was privileged to dine with the gods until he stole their nectar and ambrosia. He also tried to serve Zeus human flesh! As punishment, Tantalus had to stand in a pool of water with fruit hanging just out of reach. He couldn't eat or drink. *Look up the modern word* **tantalize** *in the dictionary.*

Princess Arachne compared her weaving skill to Athena's, so angry Athena destroyed Arachne's weaving. Fearful Arachne tried to hang herself but Athena turned her into a spider. This is why spiders spin webs. *Make up a brief story to explain why ants create anthills.*

The god Hermes guided mortals to the underworld entrance. *What would you ask a Hermes if you had the chance to talk to him?*

Pygmalion, the sculptor, sculpted an ideal woman and fell in love with her. He asked Aphrodite to send him a wife as lovely as the statue. Aphrodite brought the statue to life. Her name was Galatea. *If you could ask Aphrodite for anything, what would you ask for?*

Once, a white crow brought Athena some bad news. In her rage, Athena turned the crow black. Since then all crows have been black. *Make up a brief story to explain the color of another kind of bird.*

Zeus punished all mortals by sending curious Pandora to Earth with a box. When she opened it, all the evils of the world flew out, followed by Hope. *If you were Pandora, would you open the box? Why or why not?*

Apollo fell in love with a nymph named Daphne, who ran away from him. She asked Mother Earth to help her flee. Just as Apollo reached her, Daphne turned into a laurel tree. Apollo wears a laurel wreath in her memory. *If you were Mother Earth, how would you have helped Daphne?*

Artemis caught Actaeon watching her bathe. She turned him into a stag that her hounds hunted and killed. *Do you agree with this punishment? If not, what would be a reasonable punishment for this offense?*

Arion was a skilled musician who won many contests. Once, sailors threw him into the sea, hoping to steal his prizes. His playing had attracted many dolphins, though, and one of them took Arion home. *How has an animal helped you? Explain.*

Oracles and Omens

Imagine that you are the wise priest Nestor. You have studied the acts of the gods and goddesses and have learned to explain events that puzzle your fellow townspeople. As your neighbors come to you seeking advice, write your own interpretation of the gods' activities as you answer each of their queries. Use your knowledge and imagination!

1. Oh, will Zeus ever forgive me? I am Nellia, the fisherman's wife, and three days ago I failed to show hospitality to a beggar who came to my door. My husband has caught no fish since that day. Was the beggar a god in disguise? How can I right the wrong that I have done?

2. I am the humble shepherd Nikos, who lives in the mountains near Athens. Yesterday I lost two of my prized ewes. This morning I saw a flock of large black birds circle my usual grazing area. Tell me, Nestor, does this mean that Zeus will grant me the return of my sheep?

3. My name is Minnea. Two days ago my husband boasted that he runs faster than Hermes flies. The skies filled with jagged streaks of light and I heard a terrible roar from above. I fear that my husband has angered the gods with his boastfulness. What can I do to appease the gods?

4. I am Kalos the Unhappy. I am in love with my neighbor's daughter, but she does not return my love. Today a pair of seabirds crossed my path, gathering grass for their nest. Could this mean that Athena will favor me with my loved one's heart?

5. I am Lemnos, the old iron merchant. For years I have been the most successful merchant in the agora. Now a young iron merchant has come to steal my customers. As I walked to the marketplace this morning, I saw an old dog and a young dog fighting over a bird's carcass. Neither dog won; in fact, they each ended up with half the bird. What does this mean for my situation in the marketplace?

6. Write your own question, based on a natural event you have seen. Exchange with a classmate to answer.

Name _____   Date _____

Zeus Says: A Game of the Gods

Mount Olympus gods:
Aphrodite
Apollo
Ares
Artemis
Athena
Demeter
Dionysus
Hephaestus
Hera
Hermes
Hestia
Zeus

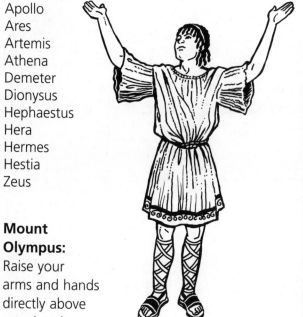

Mount Olympus:
Raise your arms and hands directly above your head.

Sky gods:
Aeon
Aether
Cronos
Eos
Helios
Hemera
Herperos
Hyperion
Narisah
Nox
Phosphorus

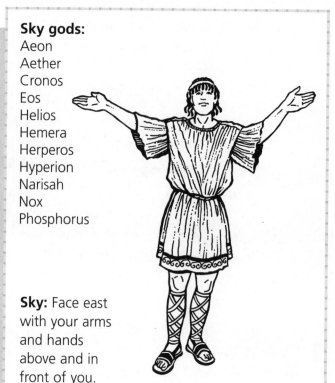

Sky: Face east with your arms and hands above and in front of you.

Marine gods:
Achelous
Acheron
Arethusa
Asterion
Eridanus
Nereus
Oceanus
Styx

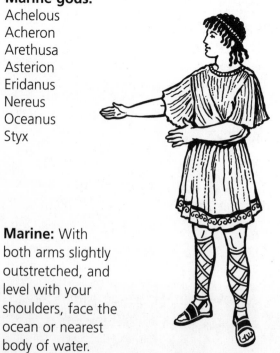

Marine: With both arms slightly outstretched, and level with your shoulders, face the ocean or nearest body of water.

Underworld gods:
Aeacos
Charon
Hades
Hypnos
Minos
Morpheus
Oneiroi
Persephone
Perseus
Sarpedon
Thanatos

Underworld: With both arms outstretched turn your palms downward.

Count on Athena!

The ancient Greeks credited Athena with the invention of numbers. The number system Athena developed used 27 letters of the Greek alphabet, including three symbols that no longer exist. The first nine letters represented the numbers 1 though 9. The second nine letters represented multiples of 10, from 10 to 90, and the final nine letters represented multiples of 100, from 100 to 900.

A	Alpha	1	I	Iota	10	P	Rho	100
B	Beta	2	K	Kappa	20	Σ	Sigma	200
Γ	Gamma	3	Λ	Lambda	30	T	Tau	300
Δ	Delta	4	M	Mu	40	Y	Upsilon	400
E	Epsilon	5	N	Nu	50	Φ	Phi	500
(obsolete)	Digamma	6	Ξ	Xi	60	X	Chi	600
Z	Zeta	7	O	Omicron	70	Ψ	Psi	700
H	Eta	8	Π	Pi	80	Ω	Omega	800
Θ	Theta	9	(obsolete)	Koppa	90	(obsolete)	Sampi	900

To write numbers that don't appear in the chart, Greeks combined the numbers, starting with the largest. For example,

$$ΛE = 35 \qquad ΣKB = 200 + 20 + 2 = 222$$

Use the chart above to write the modern equivalent of each Greek number below.

1. ΠZ =_____ **2.** ΦME = _____ **3.** ΩΠΔ = _____

Use the chart to write the Greek equivalent of each number.

4. 421 = _____ **5.** 64 = _____ **6.** 859 = _____

Count on Athena! (Continued)

Complete the following statements by translating our modern numbers into their Greek equivalents.

Ζ. _____ gods and goddesses are known as Olympians; 12 have thrones on Mount Olympus, Hades lives in the underworld, and Hestia tends the hearth.

8. The myth of Demeter and Persephone tries to explain why we have _____ seasons on Earth.

9. Athena turned Arachne into a spider with _____ legs.

Solve the following word problems by translating Greek numbers into their modern equivalents. Try to write the answers using Greek numbers.

10. Nestor has a flock of ΟΗ sheep. He hopes to sell ΛΓ in the agora on market day. If he does so, how many sheep will remain in his flock?

11. Dora's grape harvest last year weighed ΨΝΒ kilos. This year's harvest totaled ΩΛΖ kilos. How much greater was her harvest this year?

12. For the annual weeklong festival, King Kalos needs to purchase Δ loaves of bread for each of his guests. If he is expecting Ο guests, how many loaves of bread will he need to buy?

13. If there are ΙΔ bread bakers in Athens, how many loaves will each need to sell to supply King Kalos' guests?

14. At the festival, King Kalos plans to divide ΥΜΘ kilos of olives among his Ζ sons and daughters. How many kilos of olives will each receive?

15. Write your own story problem using Greek numbers. Exchange with a classmate to solve.

CHAPTER 3

Heroic Heracles

Better known to us by his Roman name, Hercules, the mythological hero Heracles was renowned among the ancient Greeks for his feats of extraordinary strength and bravery, especially the Twelve Labors that he performed to placate Zeus' wife, Hera.

Heracles

Heracles was the offspring of Zeus and the mortal Alcmene, and because of this, Hera was jealous and hated him. She tried many times to kill him, but fortunately for him, his teachers had taught him to shoot a bow and arrow, drive a chariot, and make music. When Heracles embarked on his labors—a series of difficult, dangerous tasks—in addition to his strength and bravery, he had the help of several gods and goddesses. Athena gave him a helmet and a coat of arms. His sword was a gift from Hermes. Poseidon gave him a horse, while Zeus gave him a shield. Apollo gave Heracles a bow and arrow, and Hephaestus fashioned him a golden cuirass (breastplate) and buskins (foot and leg coverings that reached to the knee) made from bronze.

Many of your students are probably familiar with the character of Hercules from the recent movie, cartoons, and books, so you may want to begin your study with a T-chart, listing on the left side what students already believe to be true about Hercules/Heracles. As you read the stories of Heracles' labors, the class can use the right side of the T-chart to list what they have learned from classical sources. (There are some similarities and many differences!)

What We Know From Modern Books and Movies:	What We Know From Classical Sources:
Heracles was married to Meg.	Heracles was married to Megara.
Heracles was called "Hercules."	Heracles is his Greek name; Hercules is the Roman name that came after.
Heracles slew many monsters.	Heracles slew many monsters.

The introduction, twelve myths, and conclusion in this chapter describe Heracles' encounters with monsters and other mythical creatures. Once students have read the introduction, they can read all the myths or just a few. You may want to have students work in small groups: each group can read one or two myths and then share the stories with the rest of the class. The Myth Cards at the end of the chapter will allow your students to share what they've read.

If your students read most or all of the Heracles stories, stop after Labor X to ask students how they think Heracles might be feeling. After ten years and ten labors, King Eurystheus told Heracles that he had two more labors to perform. Ask students what they would do if they were in Heracles' position: spend two more years risking death, or give up any hope of forgiveness.

Heracles' adventures are a natural for art projects such as murals, or for improvisational drama in the classroom. (Animal-themed paper plates work well as quick and easy animal masks.) Your students may also enjoy mock interviews with Heracles, asking him questions about his labors and his later life on Mount Olympus.

> *T*he Perseus Project (**http://www.perseus.tufts.edu/Herakles**) features an online exhibit about Heracles. The exhibit includes maps of this journey, a biography, and stories beyond the labors. If students visit the site and click on "Labors," they will find a display of ancient Greek pottery with images of the labors.

*M*ake a Mini-Book

Students keep track of Heracles' labors with their own mini-books.

MATERIALS

 🎵 The Twelve Labors of Heracles (pages 41–48)

HERE'S HOW

For each student in the class, reproduce the labors you've chosen for them to read. Direct students to cut the copied pages widthwise and staple the left sides together to make a mini-book. The left-hand (or even-numbered) pages are blank for student illustrations. They may also wish to make a cover for the booklet and illustrate.

*I*nescapable Conflict!

If your students will read several of Heracles' adventures, you may want to use these stories to introduce or review the types of literary conflict.

MATERIALS

🎵 Inescapable Conflict! reproducible (page 49)

HERE'S HOW

Reproduce the handout for each student and read aloud. Challenge students to identify each type of conflict.

Answers: 1. Character vs. Character. 2. Character vs. Nature   3. Character vs. Society 4. Character vs. Fate 5. Character vs. Self

Heracles' Conflicts

Heracles' Conflicts will reinforce student comprehension by providing examples from the labors.

MATERIALS

Heracles' Conflicts reproducible (page 50)

HERE'S HOW

Provide each student with a copy of the reproducible. Direct students to identify each type of conflict. (They may use the completed Inescapable Conflict! activity as a guide.)

Answers: 1. Character vs. Nature 2. Character vs. Character 3. Character vs. Fate 4. Character vs. Self 5. Character vs. Society

Rank the Labors

Classical writers didn't agree on the order in which Heracles faced his labors. Your students can choose a criterion and rank the labors themselves.

MATERIALS

Rank the Labors reproducible (page 51)

HERE'S HOW

Make a copy of Rank the Labors for each student or pair of students. When students have completed the worksheet, ask them to share and explain their rankings.

Make It Modern!

The labors that Hera devised sent Heracles to the ends of the ancient earth. Today, we have myths of modern monsters and knowledge of a much larger universe.

Challenge students to devise three modern labors for Heracles to complete using only his strength and ingenuity. Examples that might jump-start students' thinking include conquering Big Foot or the Loch Ness Monster, and raising the wreckage of the Titanic in only one day.

You might wish to have students illustrate their modern labors in addition to writing about them.

Extension: Ask students to use one of the modern labors they devised as the basis for a short story.

Myth Cards

Myth Cards allow students to review the Heracles stories they've already read. Or, if some students have read stories that others have not, they can use the cards as they share details of the stories with their classmates.

MATERIALS

⚖ Myth Cards (page 52)

HERE'S HOW

Provide a copy of the Myth Cards to each pair or small group of students. After students have cut out, shuffled, and piled the cards facedown, they can take turns answering the cards' questions.

Map Heracles' Journey

During the Twelve Labors, Heracles fights mythical monsters and Hera's unrelenting anger across the span of the ancient Greeks' known world. Except for the final two labors, which take Heracles to the immortals' world, the labors can be plotted on a map.

MATERIALS

⚖ Heracles' Journey reproducible (page 53)

HERE'S HOW

Provide each student (or pair of students) with a copy of Heracles' Journey and a copy of the relevant page of a modern world atlas. Have students circle each of Heracles' destinations and draw lines on the map to trace his journey. Heracles traveled by chariot and boat, so students may want to consider how they would make the same journey today.

Extensions: Ask students to calculate Heracles' mileage using a ruler and the scale given in a modern world atlas.

Using Heracles' Journey, students can create postcards for each stop Heracles made. When they've completed these, collect them in a class travel log or post them on a bulletin board.

The Twelve Labors of HERACLES

*H*eracles is better known by his Roman name, *Hercules*. He was the son of Zeus and Princess Alcmene. Born brave and incredibly strong, Heracles was also destined for trouble. But the difficulties he faced weren't his fault; in fact, Heracles' problems began even before he was born.

Zeus' wife, Hera, was terribly jealous of the other women that Zeus fell in love with. The mortal Alcmene was one of these women, and when she had Zeus' child, Hera was furious. Alcmene named the baby Heracles, which means "Hera's glory." She hoped that this gesture would satisfy Hera, but it didn't.

When Heracles was a small baby, Hera sent two fierce and deadly serpents to kill him in his crib. But Heracles surprised everyone with his amazing strength and strangled them both.

As he grew older, Heracles became famous for his strength and bravery. He met and married Megara and they had a family. But after all those years, Hera was still angry and jealous. To punish him she drove him mad. She made him believe that his wife and children were actually beasts, so he killed them all. Then Hera returned his sanity.

In despair over what he had done, Heracles asked the Oracle at Delphi how he could make up for what he'd done and overcome his guilt. The Oracle told him to offer himself as a slave to his cousin, Eurystheus, King of Mycenae.

Hera was pleased to see Heracles in such despair. "Promise him forgiveness and immortality if he completes ten tasks in ten years," she told King Eurystheus. "And I will help you devise tasks that no mortal could survive."

The weak and timid king agreed. He commanded Heracles to rid Greece of dangerous monsters, risk the immortals' wrath, and risk near-certain death. Heracles, miserable and desperate, agreed.

The Nemean Lion

"*F*irst you must kill the dreaded lion that lives in the Nemea valley," King Eurystheus instructed Heracles. Heracles paled as he considered the difficulty of the task. The huge Nemean lion had a hide so tough it couldn't be pierced with any mortal weapon. "And to prove that you killed the lion, you must bring its skin to me," Eurystheus said.

Heracles traveled to the Nemea valley, where he watched the lion from afar. He considered how best to kill it. Would his strength be enough to strangle it? With a sudden shout, Heracles chased the beast from its lair and squeezed it to death with his bare hands. He skinned the lion with its own claws, as the lion's tough hide broke Heracles' knife at the hilt. With a great heave, Heracles lifted the hide onto his back and wore it as a cloak all the way back to Eurystheus' kingdom.

When King Eurystheus saw a bloody lion striding toward him, he shuddered with fear and jumped into a brass urn to hide from the animal.

"It's me, Heracles," shouted his cousin into the urn. "The Nemean lion is dead, and my first task is complete."

The Hydra

"*N*ow you must kill the hydra who lives in the swamp of Lerna," King Eurystheus ordered Heracles. Heracles nodded, and began the long chariot ride to the swamp. As he rode to the Lernean swamp, he thought about the nine-headed hydra, a monster so poisonous that even the fumes of its breath were fatal to anyone who breathed them.

Heracles left his chariot at the edge of the swamp. He took a deep breath, deeper than any other mortal could manage, and attacked the hydra. He used his club to knock off first one head and then another. But as each head rolled to the marshy earth, two new heads grew from each empty neck.

"Bring me my firebrand," Heracles called to his chariot driver as he struggled with the monster. When the driver handed him the burning torch, Heracles was able to sear each empty neck closed, so no new heads could grow.

From Mount Olympus, Hera watched Heracles' victory and was filled with anger. In an attempt to stop him, she sent a giant crab to earth to pinch his heels. With a swift kick, Heracles sent the crab flying. Then he spilled some of the hydra's blood onto the ground and dipped his arrows in the puddle, making them as poisonous as the hydra itself. Satisfied, Heracles turned to his chariot driver.

"Back to the king," he directed his driver. "And on to the next task."

The Sword-Tusked Boar

Hera visited King Eurystheus in his palace. She strode toward him angrily.

"Make Heracles' tasks harder!" she shouted. "They're too easy for him now. Make him labor through this punishment. And if he should meet a monster he can't defeat . . ." Hera laughed bitterly. "So much the better!"

Timid King Eurystheus nodded and listened to Hera's suggestions. When Heracles returned to the palace, Eurystheus offered the most difficult challenge yet.

"Now you must trap the Erymanthian boar," he told Heracles. Heracles nodded and traveled to the slopes of Mount Erymanthus. There lived a wild boar whose tusks were as sharp as the finest swords. To approach the wily animal directly would mean certain death.

Heracles peered into the animal's cave. Covering his ears, he shouted a terrible shout that echoed throughout the cave. Terrified, the boar ran outside. Heracles chased it to the snowy top of the mountain, where he drove it into a snowbank. Stuck in the snowbank with its own tusks, the beast couldn't move. Heracles chained the boar by its middle and dragged it to the gates of King Eurystheus' palace. The boar's deafening roars scared the king, who hid again in the brass urn until he was ready to send Heracles away on the next task.

The Brass Birds

Lake Stymphalus was home to a swarm of deadly birds. Although they resembled cranes, the Stymphalides had razorlike claws and beaks that the birds used to tear apart and eat mortal flesh. Their pointed brass feathers were so sharp that if one feather fell from a bird in flight, it killed anyone standing below it.

"Get rid of those birds," King Eurystheus demanded of Heracles.

Heracles set off for Lake Stymphalus, covering himself completely with the skin of the Nemean lion that he still wore as a cloak. When the flock of birds saw Heracles, they stared hungrily at him. As if they were one huge bird, the flock swooped down upon him. Their claws slid from the slick lion's fur and their swordlike beaks failed to penetrate the lion's thick skin. Frustrated, the birds cried louder and louder and tried again and again to reach the mortal they knew to be hidden under the fur.

Suddenly, Heracles gave a gigantic roar that first silenced and then terrified the birds. Scared of the noisy invader, the birds flew away from Lake Stymphalus, never to return. Heracles returned to Mycenae to learn of his next labor.

The Sacred Deer

*F*rom her throne on Mount Olympus, Hera watched Heracles' success with growing frustration. "Harder, more dangerous labors!" she cried to herself. When her eye fell on Artemis, the goddess of the hunt, she had a brilliant idea. She descended from Mount Olympus to whisper it in King Eurystheus' ear.

When Heracles next greeted King Eurystheus, he noticed the steely glint in his cousin's eye and knew the next task might be impossible.

"Artemis has a herd of sacred deer," began the king.

Heracles nodded. Like all mortals, he knew of Artemis' deep devotion to her animals and the dreadful punishments she inflicted on those who hurt them.

"Bring the stag back to me," ordered King Eurystheus, "alive."

Heracles traveled many weeks to the Ceryneia forest where Artemis' herd of sacred deer roamed. When he found them, Heracles spent many more weeks simply watching the deer. King Eurystheus hoped that Heracles' brute strength would harm a deer and call Artemis' wrath down upon him. Heracles knew this, so he waited patiently before he approached the animals.

Among the herd, standing taller than the rest, was the Cerynean stag. Heracles knew him by his golden antlers and brazen hooves. Slowly, Heracles approached the stag. When the stag was accustomed to Heracles, the man and the deer ran together through the forest to the gates of King Eurystheus' palace.

Eurystheus had not expected to see Heracles alive again. After a glance at his cousin's startled face, Heracles led the animal back to its herd in the forest. Then he returned to Mycenae to learn the next labor.

Cleaning the Augean Stables

*E*urystheus wanted to shame Heracles into giving up the labors, so he devised a task that he hoped would humble his cousin. King Augeas, who lived across the mountains to the west, in the land of Elis, had a herd of 3,000 cattle whose stables had not been cleaned in 30 years.

"You have one day to clean the Augean stables," Eurystheus told Heracles with a laugh. The king was certain that the stables couldn't be cleaned in a year and so was Augeas. When he greeted Heracles at the stable door, Augeas laughed at Heracles, too.

"If you can clean these stables in one day," said King Augeas, flinging open the stable doors, "I'll give you one tenth of my herd of cattle."

Heracles stared in dismay at the mountains of dung—30 years' worth—that filled the stable. The two kings were right: no mortal man could clean the stable alone, not in one day, maybe not in a lifetime. So Heracles needed to find another way.

Heracles walked to the place where the Alpheus and the Peleus rivers met. Using his enormous strength, Heracles held back the water with one hand while he pushed the rivers' banks with the other. He pushed again and again until the course of the two rivers ran straight through King Augeas's stables. Heracles released the water he had held back and watched as it surged into and then out of the stables, washing away the mounds of dung.

Satisfied, Heracles washed himself in the rivers and returned to his cousin's palace.

Visit to the Amazons

*F*or his next labor, Eurystheus decided to send Heracles far away.

"Heracles," he instructed his cousin, "travel east to the land of the Amazons. From there, you must bring me the golden girdle of Hippolyta, Queen of the Amazons." The girdle was a belt that signified her status as queen.

The Amazons were a tribe of women who waged war more skillfully than any group of mortals. They were known to dislike men. King Eurystheus and Heracles both knew that it would take more than brute strength to survive a visit to the Amazons.

Heracles traveled many weeks to reach the tribe's land east of Phrygia. He hoped to approach the Amazons as a guest and fellow warrior. How he would get Hippolyta's girdle, though, he didn't know.

To his surprise, the great Queen Hippolyta greeted Heracles warmly as a warrior equal to herself. She admired his strength and offered him her girdle willingly. Hippolyta even agreed to marry Heracles, but watchful Hera intervened. Disguised as an Amazon, Hera spread a rumor among the tribe that Heracles had come to kidnap the queen. The Amazons attacked Heracles. Skillful warrior that he was, Heracles was able to escape with the girdle. Sadly, Queen Hippolyta had been killed in battle, and Heracles returned to Mycenae alone to give the girdle to the king.

Diomedes' Horses

*K*ing Eurystheus, who was growing weary of Heracles, decided to send him even farther away.

"Go to Thrace, a kingdom far north of here," Eurystheus ordered Heracles. "There, King Diomedes keeps his man-eating horses. Bring them back to me alive."

Heracles traveled to Thrace, where he found the four mares who were famous for feeding on human flesh. They bared their blood-stained teeth at him when Heracles approached. Heracles knew that only an evil man could breed such evil horses, so he slew Diomedes and fed his remains to the four horses. Suddenly, the horses became so tame that Heracles was able to ride them back to Mycenae.

Eurystheus was surprised by Heracles' swift return and he was scared of the horses. He leaped into his brass urn to hide. From within the urn, he ordered his servants to dedicate the horses to Hera. Hera set them free on Mount Olympus. Now too tame to defend themselves, the mares were eaten by Apollo's wild beasts. In the meantime, King Eurystheus was thinking of an even more dangerous task for his cousin.

A Fire-Breathing Bull

Eurystheus sent Heracles south for his next task. "Capture the Cretan Bull," he commanded his cousin. "Bring it back alive or don't come back at all."

Heracles traveled to King Minos's kingdom on the island of Crete, far to the south of Mycenae. There he saw the gigantic Cretan Bull. It was a fierce, fire-breathing creature that Poseidon had given to King Minos as a gift and a curse.

"Even we," the Cretans told Heracles, "skilled bullfighters that we are, can't capture this bull."

Heracles ignored them and seized the angry bull by its great horns. He flung it to the ground and dragged it many miles until it was tame. Then he rode it back to King Eurystheus' palace in Mycenae.

When he saw his cousin riding the gigantic bull, the cowardly king hid again in his brass urn.

"Take that animal away," he bellowed.

Heracles hauled the bull to the plains of Marathon, where he allowed it to roam freely. It became known as the Marathonian Bull and was later killed by the warrior Theseus.

The Monster's Cattle

"Bring me the cattle of Geryon," shouted King Eurystheus from within his brass urn. Heracles knew that the large, red cows lived at Gades, an island in the middle of the seas. The island and the cattle were guarded by the three-headed monster named Geryon and his two-headed dog, Eurythion. Eurystheus was certain that Heracles couldn't possibly reach the island, let alone survive an encounter with the monster.

But Heracles traveled quickly to the end of the known world, where he spied the golden boat of Helios, the sun, floating in the ocean. With his powerful bow and poisoned arrow, Heracles took aim at the sun and called to Helios.

"If you don't lend me your ship I will shoot you from the sky," Heracles shouted at the sky. The frightened sun agreed.

As Heracles prepared to sail to Geryon's island, he raised the mountains Abiya and Calpe to serve as landmarks on his return trip.

As he sailed to Gades, waves threatened to overturn Heracles' ship. Again, Heracles raised his bow and arrow. The scared waves subsided and Heracles reached the island.

He began to load the cattle onto his boat immediately. When Geryon attacked him, Heracles sent a poisoned arrow through all three of the monster's heads.

When Heracles reached the mainland, Hera attacked the cattle with a swarm of gadflies that chased the herd all over Greece. But Heracles patiently rounded them up and brought them to King Eurystheus.

Exhausted from his labors, Heracles demanded food, rest, and his freedom.

"You may eat with the servants," said King Eurystheus, "and then I will release you."

Heracles ate and waited to be freed.

Hera Gets Involved Again

King Eurystheus sacrificed the cattle of Geryon to Hera. As he did so, the goddess appeared to him.

"Heracles' labors are complete," said King Eurystheus wearily. "I must grant him forgiveness and release him from service, just as the Oracle foretold."

"You will not do any such thing," Hera exclaimed. "Didn't Heracles have help from his chariot driver when he killed the hydra? And Heracles didn't clean the stables; the rivers did! He has two more labors to perform, and I have saved the hardest for last."

King Eurystheus agreed to assign Heracles two more labors, but he sent a servant to inform his cousin. When Heracles confronted the king, he found Eurystheus once again hiding in his urn.

"I will do two more of your foolish errands," said Heracles angrily. "Not to please you, but because I still seek the gods' forgiveness for my madness. And my labors have won me great glory all over Greece, which pleases the gods."

Eurystheus sighed with relief from within his urn and prepared to send Heracles on his next labor.

LABOR XI
Three Golden Apples

"In the garden of the Hesperides," said King Eurystheus, "you will find the apple tree that Mother Earth gave to Hera when she married Zeus. Bring me three apples from that tree."

Heracles set off uncertainly, for no mortal knew where the garden was located. At last, Heracles met Nereus, the Old Man of the Sea, who knew the secret. Heracles used his great strength to squeeze the secret out of Nereus: "The garden, which is owned by the Titan Atlas, lies west of the setting sun."

On the way to the garden, Heracles found the Titan Prometheus chained to the Caucasus Mountains. Heracles released Prometheus, and Prometheus warned him that the apples would be fatal to any mortal who tried to pick them.

When Heracles reached the garden, he saw Atlas holding up the sky. "That looks very heavy," Heracles remarked. Zeus had long ago sentenced Atlas to hold the sky on his shoulders as a punishment. "I would be happy to hold Earth for a while if you will pick me three apples," Heracles said, as if he had just thought of the idea.

"I'll do it," said Atlas enthusiastically, for Earth was a heavy burden. He handed Earth to Heracles and picked three golden apples from Hera's tree.

"Maybe I'll keep these apples for myself," said Atlas, walking away from Heracles. Heracles realized that, now that he was free of the heavy Earth, Atlas would never return.

"Fine," said Heracles hastily. "Hold the sky while I make a pad for my shoulders from this lion skin. Then I will hold Earth again."

Atlas agreed, and when he again shouldered Earth, Heracles picked up the apples and ran to Mycenae.

Heracles gave the apples to his cousin, who gave them to Athena. She returned them to the garden of the Hesperides, since they would shrivel and rot in the mortal world.

Capturing Cerberus

"Capture Cerberus from the underworld and bring him here alive," Eurystheus ordered Heracles. The king dreaded the sight of the three-headed watchdog of Hades, but Hera had commanded him to assign Heracles this most dangerous labor.

Heracles searched Earth until he found an entrance to the underworld far in the west, near Helios's evening palace. To capture the monstrous dog, Heracles twisted the features of his face into a hideous expression and walked into the underworld. Hades was so frightened by the sight of Heracles' face that he handed him the dog.

"Treat Cerberus well," begged Hades, as Heracles left the underworld. Cerberus allowed Heracles to drag him into the upper world and as far as the gates of King Eurystheus' palace.

Again hiding in his urn, King Eurystheus shouted to his cousin. "You are free from my service and forgiven for your madness. Now take the beast away."

Heracles was relieved to be finished with his labors, but he still feared the gods. Mindful of what Hades had asked, Heracles dragged Cerberus all the way back home to the underworld. Then, after 10 years and 12 labors, Heracles was free.

What Happened Next to Heracles?

At the end of his labors, Heracles was only 28 years old. He had a long life ahead of him. For many years, he traveled around Greece performing heroic deeds.

Unfortunately, Hera was still angry at Heracles and she again made him insane. Heracles killed many men and again had to atone for his misdeeds. This time Zeus determined Heracles' punishment and sentenced him to serve three years as the queen of Lydia's slave. Queen Omphale dressed Heracles in women's clothes and commanded him to spin and sew while she wore his lion skin and used his weapons. When Heracles was released, he again traveled through Greece performing feats of strength and daring.

Heracles suffered terribly when he was stabbed by his own arrow and poisoned by the hydra's blood. Too strong to be killed by the poison, he ordered his friends to build a funeral pyre where he could lie down and die. Heracles gave away his weapons and climbed onto the fire. As the flames touched his feet, his servants heard sudden thunder and saw Heracles disappear. Zeus had called Heracles to Mount Olympus, where he became an immortal.

The gods welcomed Heracles, for the fates had predicted an attack from a terrible enemy. When the 50-legged giants surrounded Mount Olympus, Heracles cast them into the dark pit of Tartarus. This was Heracles' final heroic deed; afterward, he lived in happiness, married to Hebe, the goddess of eternal youth.

Inescapable Conflict!

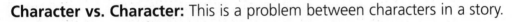

Conflict, a problem or struggle between opposing forces, is the engine that drives a story from its beginning to its conclusion. A conflict is usually introduced early on in the story and is often resolved at the end. You have probably seen many examples of conflict in the Greek myths you've already read.

There are five basic types of literary conflict. As you read the description of each, list an example from the Greek myths you know.

Character vs. Character: This is a problem between characters in a story.

Character vs. Himself or Herself: This is a problem within a character's own mind.

Character vs. Society: This is a problem between a character and the larger world in which he or she lives (school, traditions, the law).

Character vs. Nature: This is a problem between a character and an element of nature.

Character vs. Fate: This is a problem beyond the character's control.

For each of the following situations, decide which of the five types of conflict is being described.

1. Apollo and Ares argued over whose horses run faster.

_____

2. Paris the shepherd fought his way down Mount Ida through a hailstorm.

_____

3. Jessa wanted to fight in the Trojan War, but girls in Greece weren't supposed to be warriors.

_____

4. Kaliope was changed into a grasshopper, though she hoped to become a butterfly.

_____

5. Darna wanted to climb Mount Ida, but first she had to overcome her fear of heights.

_____

Below, give an example of a conflict using characters you know from a Greek myth. Afterward, exchange your conflict with a classmate and see if each of you can identify the type of conflict the other described.

Heracles' Conflicts

Throughout his Twelve Labors, Heracles encountered many monsters, mortals, and difficult situations. Altogether, these encounters add up to a lively story that the ancient Greeks enjoyed hearing again and again.

Use your knowledge of literary conflict to identify the type of conflict Heracles faced in each of the following situations.

1. Great waves tried to overturn Heracles as he sailed to the island of Gades.

_____

2. King Augeas challenged Heracles to clean his stables in one day.

_____

3. Heracles was cursed from birth to do terrible things while under Hera's spell.

_____

4. Heracles asked himself how to best attack the Nemean lion.

_____

5. When Heracles killed Megara, he broke the law and had to be punished.

_____

Write five examples of your own from the Heracles stories.

1. _____

_____

2. _____

_____

3. _____

_____

4. _____

_____

5. _____

_____

Rank the Labors

With Hera's help, King Eurystheus assigned Heracles tasks that seemed nearly impossible. And with each of Heracles' successes, the king tried to think of an even more difficult task.

Imagine that you are facing Heracles' labors, but you can choose the order in which you do them. Would you choose the worst to do first? And what do you think is more difficult or dangerous, cleaning the Augean stables or capturing the watchdog of the underworld?

Listed below are Hercules' labors in order. Next to them, write the order in which you would take on the labors. Then, on another sheet of paper, explain your decisions.

Heracles' Labors   _____'s Labors

1. Bringing the Nemean Lion Skin to the king _____

2. Killing the hydra _____

3. Trapping the Sword-Tusked Boar _____

4. Scaring Away the Brass Birds _____

5. Capturing the Cerynean Stag _____

6. Cleaning the Augean Stables _____

7. Visiting the Amazons _____

8. Bringing Diomedes' Horses to the King _____

9. Capturing the Cretan Bull _____

10. Bringing the Cattle of Geryon to the king _____

11. Gathering Hera's Apples _____

12. Capturing Cerberus _____

What title would you give the myth that you read?

Who was your favorite character? Describe him or her and explain why this was your favorite.

Who was your least favorite character? Describe him or her and explain why this was your least favorite.

If you faced a challenge similar to Heracles', what would you do?

What part of the myth was the most exciting to you? Why?

Myths often show examples of good vs. bad. In the myth you read, who was good? Who was bad? Explain.

Describe a conflict between two characters in this myth.

As an ancient Greek listening to this myth, what might you learn about immortals?

What do you consider Heracles' most difficult labor? Why?

As a modern student reading this myth, what did you learn about the ancient Greeks?

If you had to perform Heracles' labors, what one modern item would you wish for to help you? Why?

The ancient Greeks admired Heracles as a great hero. What are two of his heroic qualities?

If Hera told you to assign Heracles a thirteenth labor, what would it be?

Ask and answer your own question.

Heracles' Journey

Heracles traveled far and wide to complete his labors. Except for the final two, which took him to the immortals' world, the places Heracles visited can be found on a map. Use the list below to check off the places he visited as you find them on the map that your teacher gives you. To calculate mileage, remember that he returned to King Eurystheus' palace in Mycenae after every labor.

- [ ] Heracles began his trip by visiting the Oracle at Delphi.

- [ ] The Oracle directed him to Mycenae.

- [ ] Heracles fought the lion in Nemea.

- [ ] Heracles killed the hydra in Lerna.

- [ ] Heracles found the sacred deer in Ceryneia.

- [ ] The boar was on the Erymanthus mountain.

- [ ] King Augeas' stables were in Elis.

- [ ] The birds were at Stymphalos, the name of the lake and the nearby town.

- [ ] Heracles captured the bull in Crete.

- [ ] The mares of Diomedes were in Thrace.

- [ ] Heracles is believed to have sought the Amazons in Mysia.

- [ ] The cattle of Geryon were captured in Erythia.

CHAPTER 4

Who Started the Trojan War?

We have the great poet Homer to thank for the immortal legend of the Trojan War. Most historians now believe that a trade war actually did take place in Asia Minor some time around 1250 BC. The Mycenaeans, the Greeks Homer described in *The Iliad* (*Ilium* is another name for Troy) and *The Odyssey*, were suffering from poor harvests and famine. Groups of Mycenaeans went on raids overseas, and such raids may have provoked the Trojan War.

In the 1870s, an amateur archaeologist named Heinrich Schliemann determined to find the ruins of Troy. Following Homer's description of where the walled city once stood, Schliemann dug at Hisarlik in Turkey. He uncovered the ruins of several cities, many of which had been destroyed as if by war. Historians now believe that Troy was a real place and that at least one Trojan War took place.

Aphrodite

Homer's epics tell the story of large-scale mortal and immortal conflict and cooperation. The events that led to the war, the Trojan War itself, and the aftermath involve nearly every Olympian god, countless lesser gods, and many fascinating monsters.

All the troubles began at the only known wedding between a mortal and an immortal. The play "The Apple of Discord" will introduce your students to Homer's version of how the Trojan War began.

A Read-Aloud Play: "The Apple of Discord"

MATERIALS

🎵 "The Apple of Discord" reproducible (pages 59–62)

HERE'S HOW

Reproduce the handout for each student and read aloud. Challenge students to identify each type of conflict.

Before assigning parts, introduce students to the function of the Chorus. The Chorus in Greek drama played a role much like a modern narrator or the color commentator at a sporting event. That is, the Chorus told the audience the setting, revealed the action, and often explained the motives of the characters. The Chorus's role was also to remind the audience of the drama's moral. Usually, the moral was about treating the immortals with great respect!

Read through the list of characters and assign parts. Note: In this play, the role of the Chorus has been divided into Chorus 1 and Chorus 2 to allow more students to participate. Since the Chorus was usually a group of actors, try to assign at least two students to each Chorus role.

If you choose to act out this play fully, you may want to see Make a Mask (page 75) or Dress Greek! (page 75). A Golden Delicious apple is a perfect prop, but if this is unavailable, wrap a tennis ball (or other ball that bounces) in foil and then yellow food wrap. This dramatic prop can then be tossed into the group of wedding guests without falling apart.

Book Links

To delve further into Homer's *Iliad* and *Odyssey*, check out these books for young readers:

Dateline: Troy by Paul Fleischman. New York: Scholastic, 1996

The Iliad retold by Ian Strachen. New York: Kingfisher, 1997

The Children's Homer: The Adventures of Odysseus and the Tale of Troy by Padraic Colum. New York: Aladdin, 1982

The Wanderings of Odysseus: The Story of the Odyssey by Rosemary Sutcliff. New York: Delacorte, 1996

The judgment of Paris led to conflict between the Olympians. Throughout the war, many of the gods and goddesses favored one side or the other. From reading this play, your students may be able to predict which side Hera, Athena, and Aphrodite favored. The following list is a helpful reference.

Favored the Greeks: Hera, Athena, Poseidon, Hermes, Hephaestus

Favored the Trojans: Aphrodite, Apollo, Ares, Artemis

Neutral: Demeter, Hades, Hestia, Zeus

Whodunnit? and Wanted!

References to the Judgment of Paris and Helen's abduction to Troy appear as often in modern literature as in ancient myths. Tennyson, Yeats, and, more recently, W. S. Merwin are a few examples of modern writers who have taken Paris and Helen as their topics. Many writers have blamed or credited one character or another with starting the conflict.

After reading "The Apple of Discord" your students can consider each character's role in the conflict that became the Trojan War.

HERE'S HOW

1. Ask students to consider a hypothetical conflict: Sam punched Kathryn on the bus. Ask students who is to blame for the conflict that results.

2. Now explain you forgot to mention that Kathryn tripped Sam as he was climbing the steps of the bus. Ask students who is now responsible for the conflict.

3. Tell students that yesterday Lily told Kathryn that Sam planned to punch her. Ask students who is responsible now. Ask them if it matters whether Lily was telling the truth or not.

4. Point out to students that they have just experienced how difficult conflicts can be to untangle. Explain that many writers have tried to blame the Trojan War on the actions or inactions of a single character. Your students' challenge is to determine for themselves who was to blame.

5. Direct a student to read aloud the instructions on the Whodunnit? reproducible. Then have students complete the activity. Allow them to use another sheet of paper if they need more room.. You may wish to model one response. An example follows:

Thetis and Pelus were responsible because they should have invited Eris to the wedding. They were not responsible because they were minding their own business at the wedding.

6. Explain to students that they will complete the Wanted! poster for the character or characters they determine to be most responsible for starting the Trojan War. These posters make a good display for the hall or bulletin board.

Answers: Answers will vary.

Tales From Troy

"Tales from Troy" (pages 65–66) tells the story of Achilles and his mother, the goddess Thetis, whose wedding was the setting for "The Apple of Discord." It also introduces students to some memorable Greeks and Trojans.

After students read this story, you may wish to have them illustrate scenes, act out sections, or rewrite it as a first-person narrative, choosing any of the many characters as the storyteller.

Discussion idea: Ask students how this story agrees or disagrees with what they have learned of the Greek idea of fate.

Homer's Heroes

Memorable descriptions helped Homer's listeners keep straight the characters in his epics. Distribute copies of Homer's Heroes (page 67) and have students practice writing similes and metaphors about some famous characters from *The Iliad*.

Make a Trojan Horse

The Trojan Horse, also called the Wooden Horse, is the symbol of the Trojan War. Just as the Greeks constructed the horse from the wood of their ships, students can craft horses from easily found materials.

MATERIALS

- Make a Trojan Horse worksheets (pages 68–69)
  (two copies of page 69, photocopied on card stock, for each student)
- drinking straws (at least one per student, but extras are handy)
- wagon wheel pasta (at least four wheels per student, but extras are handy)
- decorative materials such as markers, glitter, google eyes, foil, etc.
- scissors
- hole punch
- ruler

◀ *a completed Trojan horse, ready to decorate*

HERE'S HOW

1. Have students gather the necessary materials. You may want to list on the board what each student should have on his or her desk.

2. Encourage students to decorate their horses creatively. The Trojan Horse was described simply as "large," and students can interpret the horse any way they wish.

3. When horses are complete, students can create descriptive labels for them, as in a museum. Create dioramas or a classroom display of Trojan Horses.

Note: Photocopy the Trojan Horse pattern pieces onto the heaviest cardstock your copier will permit.

Extension: Direct students to write letters to the people of Troy explaining what the horse is and why they should accept the gift. Students can explain to the Trojans why the decoration of their horses will especially please the goddess Athena.

On the Way to Ithaka

Homer's *Odyssey* tells the story of its hero Odysseus and his struggles to return home to Ithaka after the Trojan War. Traditionally, epic heroes are characters who are remembered for both their words and deeds. Odysseus is brave, but he is also known for his quickness and intelligence. The story of Odysseus' meeting with the Cyclops Polyphemus in Book 9 of *The Odyssey* illustrates both of these characteristics.

MATERIALS

⸎ On the Way to Ithaka reproducible (page 70)

HERE'S HOW

1. Explain to students that in Homer's epic, Odysseus wanders for ten years, encountering various villains and dangers, as he tries to get home after the fall of Troy. One such adventure is recounted in "On the Way to Ithaka."

2. Distribute copies of "On the Way to Ithaka" to students. After they read the story, ask them to give examples of what Odysseus does and says that makes him a hero. You may want to make class lists on the chalkboard with the following headings:

What Odysseus Does   What Odysseus Says

Extension: Invite students to write a short essay that begins "If I were Odysseus, I would have . . ." Students can pick up the thread of the narrative at any point in the story. Some students may prefer to write a short essay that begins "If I were Odysseus, I wouldn't have . . ."

Everyday Greek

MATERIALS

⸎ Everyday Greek reproducible (page 71)

Once students become aware of the Greek roots of modern expressions, they may suddenly hear them all the time.

HERE'S HOW

Ask students, for example, if they or anyone they know has ever pulled an "Achilles tendon," or read of a businessperson with a "Midas touch." And nearly everyone has heard of the ship named Titanic; now your students will know the source of her name.

Who Started the Trojan War?

The poet Homer, whose name means "blind poet," described the Trojan War and its aftermath in his two great epic poems, *The Iliad* and *The Odyssey*. Today, most historians believe that Troy was a real place, and they also believe that a trade war took place sometime around 1250 BC. But we also know that much of what Homer wrote was not true but was based on myth. For instance, the stories feature lots of interaction between mortals and immortals.

Legend has it that the war got its start at the only wedding between a goddess and a mortal, Thetis and King Peleus. Some blame Aphrodite, the goddess of beauty and love, for starting the war. Others hold Helen, Queen of Sparta, accountable for the trouble that resulted. Read the story below and decide for yourself who was to blame for starting the Trojan War.

The Apple of Discord

*You are invited to the wedding of Thetis, daughter of the sea god Nereus,
and King Peleus, King of the Myrmidions. . . .*

CHARACTERS

Eris: Goddess of discord

Zeus: King of all the gods

Hera: Zeus' wife; goddess of marriage and protector of women

Athena: Goddess of beauty and wisdom

Aphrodite: Goddess of love and beauty

Hermes: Messenger of the gods

Paris: Shepherd and son of Queen Hecuba and King Priam of Troy

Menelaus: King of Sparta and Helen's husband

Helen: Queen of Sparta and Menelaus's wife; considered the most beautiful woman in the world

Chorus 1

Chorus 2

Servant

Scene 1

At the wedding of Thetis and King Peleus

Chorus 1:   Welcome to the wedding of Thetis and King Peleus. Nearly all the gods and goddesses are here. Only Eris, the goddess of discord, was not invited because the bride and groom feared her spite would ruin their celebration. True to her nature, Eris bursts angrily into the wedding hall.

The Apple of Discord (Continued)

Chorus 2: The guests are curious and fearful. Why did Eris come?

Eris: Thetis! King Peleus! Brothers and sisters! Here is your wedding gift from me, and may you forever regret insulting me by leaving me off the guest list.

Chorus 1: Eris throws a golden apple into the crowd of wedding guests and storms out. On the apple is written "For the fairest." Three goddesses step forward to claim the apple.

Chorus 2: The goddesses glare spitefully at one another.

Aphrodite: The apple is for me! I am the goddess of love and beauty, so no goddess or mortal is fairer than I.

Athena: But as the goddess of wisdom, I am wise enough to recognize my own description. "The fairest." That's me.

Hera: As the wife of Zeus, protector of women, and goddess of marriage, I am clearly the chosen goddess. The apple is mine.

Chorus 1: The goddesses and the wedding guests look imploringly at Zeus, hoping that he will settle the dispute and let the celebration continue. But Zeus doesn't want to decide because he fears the anger of the two goddesses who aren't chosen.

Chorus 2: Zeus has an idea.

Zeus: Aha! Paris, the lonely shepherd on Mount Ida, will choose which goddess is the fairest. Hermes, deliver the goddesses and the apple to Paris and let him decide. The rest of us will stay here and celebrate.

Scene 2
. . . .
A lonely hillside on Mount Ida

Chorus 1: Paris was not always a shepherd. He was born to King Priam and Queen Hecuba of Troy. When Paris was born, a soothsayer predicted that he would cause the downfall of Troy. The soothsayer left him on a hill to die, but he was rescued by a bear and raised by a herdsman. He became a shepherd himself, and spent long days tending his sheep on the mountain.

Chorus 2: Paris is very surprised when Hermes appears with three goddesses and hands him a golden apple.

Hermes: Zeus has decided that you must choose the fairest of these three goddesses. Give the apple to the most beautiful.

The Apple of Discord (Continued)

Paris: I am a shepherd, and I know nothing of immortal beauty.

Hermes: Zeus has commanded this, and you must obey.

Hera: I will help you to decide, young Paris. If you choose me, I will shower you with power and wealth for the rest of your mortal life.

Athena: But I, handsome shepherd, will grant you success in war. You will be a hero whose daring adventures will be told and retold forever. Choose me.

Aphrodite: I offer so little, dear Paris, next to wealth and heroism. If you choose me, I can only promise you the most beautiful woman in the world as your wife. Endless beauty and love is what I offer.

**Choruses
1 and 2:** Which goddess will he choose? Paris thinks and thinks while the goddesses wait and wait.

Paris: I have decided. Keep your promise, Aphrodite, for I have chosen you.

**Hera and
Athena:** You will regret this, wretched Paris!

Aphrodite: Her name is Helen, Queen of Sparta. Go to the court of Menelaus of Sparta and she will be yours.

Scene 3

Sparta

Chorus 1: Many years passed before Aphrodite kept her promise. Paris returned to Troy, where King Priam and Queen Hecuba, relieved to see their son alive, welcomed him home. King Priam asked Paris to go to Troy, to rescue Priam's sister, Princess Hesione, who had been kidnapped years before. Paris sailed for Troy, but Aphrodite had other plans.

Aphrodite: *(speaking to the audience)* Now I will fulfill my promise to the shepherd who chose me as the fairest. I will blow his ship off course and send him to Sparta, where Helen lives with her husband, King Menelaus. I never told Paris that Helen was already married, did I?

Chorus 2: Paris reaches Sparta and meets Helen, the most beautiful woman in the world. He learns that Helen is the daughter of Zeus and Leda, the former Queen of Sparta. He also discovers that she is already married to Menelaus, but he is so swayed by her beauty that he doesn't care.

The Apple of Discord (Continued)

Paris: Come away with me to Troy, Helen. I love you and I know that Aphrodite, the goddess of love, wouldn't think it wrong. Marry me!

Helen: I will go with you, Paris. I have never loved my husband, Menelaus, and I do love you. Let's go today while Menelaus is away in Crete.

Aphrodite: *(speaking to the audience)* I will favor the couple with gentle winds to send their ship home to Troy.

Scene 4

Sparta

Chorus 1: Menelaus discovers Helen's absence, and a servant explains what happened.

Servant: Helen and Paris left together, taking many of the palace treasures. We couldn't stop them, though we tried. If was as if they had the power of an immortal helping them to leave!

Menelaus: I love my wife and I want her back. And this is a grave insult to me and to all of Sparta. This means war! I will tell my brother, King Agamemnon, to raise an army of Greek men. We'll sail to Troy and battle for Helen's return. Even if it takes a thousand ships and ten years, we will conquer the Trojans.

Scene 5

Mount Olympus

Chorus 2: Meanwhile, on Mount Olympus, Eris watches Menelaus in his castle, and Paris and Helen sailing across the Aegean Sea.

Eris: My plan is working splendidly! The Trojan War will be the bloodiest, longest, most harrowing war ever fought. Every god, goddess, and mortal will regret offending me.

Chorus 1: Eris's prediction was correct. The Trojan War dragged on for ten years, and cost many lives. Paris was killed in battle, but not before the soothsayer's prediction came true: his return led to Troy's ruin.

Chorus 2: After the Greeks destroyed Troy, Helen was captured and returned to Menelaus. He still loved his wife, and he took Helen back to Sparta.

**Choruses
1 and 2:** Treat the immortals with respect or risk their wrath.

Whodunnit?

After reading "The Apple of Discord," think about who was to blame for starting the Trojan War. Many gods, goddesses, and mortals took part in the events that led to the war, but was one more responsible than the others?

   Next to each character's name below, list the reasons you believe he or she is responsible for the conflict that led to the Trojan War. Then list reasons he or she isn't responsible for starting the war. (Use another sheet of paper if necessary.) After you have completed the chart and discussed your answers with the class, decide who you think is most to blame. Fill in the Wanted! poster on page 64 with that character's name, an illustration, and the reasons you think he or she bears the most blame for starting the Trojan War.

Character	Why I think this character was responsible for the conflict.	Why I think this character wasn't responsible for the conflict.
Thetis and Peleus		
Zeus		
Eris		
Helen		
Aphrodite		
Hera		
Athena		
Paris		
Menelaus		
Hermes		

WANTED!

_____

stands accused of starting the **Trojan War**

Evidence against this character includes:

_____

_____

_____

_____

_____

_____

Tales From Troy

*T*he centaur Chiron approached the goddess Thetis. "I've come to talk about your son Achilles," he began.

Thetis studied the half-man, half-horse for a moment. She knew that he was old and learned.

"My prediction is this," said the centaur. "The Greek army will need Achilles to capture Troy. He will be a hero, but he will die there."

Thetis knew Chiron's predictions were truthful, but she determined to fight fate as well as she could.

When Achilles was a baby, Thetis had held him by one tiny heel and dipped him into the River Styx, the magical river that separates Earth from the underworld. Though Achilles was half-mortal, Thetis wanted to guarantee her son's immortality by dipping him in the water. Still, despite having taken this precaution, she was worried by what the old centaur told her. So just to be safe, she disguised him and hid him among the daughters of King Lycomedes on the island of Skyros so he would be free from harm.

Meanwhile, Greek troops were preparing to wage war on Troy. Two leaders of the Greek forces, Agamemnon and Odysseus, heard a rumor that the skilled young warrior Achilles was hiding on Skyros. Odysseus volunteered to find him.

Odysseus arrived at the court of King Lycomedes with glittering jewels and other gifts for his host and his many daughters. Odysseus watched the king's daughters eyeing the gifts, all except for the tallest daughter who showed no interest in the treasures. Odysseus shifted the jewels to reveal the hilt of a gleaming sword. Suddenly the tallest daughter leapt forward to grab it. As she did, Odysseus recognized who it was and called out, "Achilles!"

The spell that Thetis had placed on Achilles was broken. At the sound of his name, he remembered who he was and agreed to go with Odysseus to fight in the war at Troy.

Once in Troy, Agamemnon offended Achilles, and Achilles refused to fight. Instead, his good friend Patroklos put on Achilles' armor and fought in his place. The armor was good, but Patroklos was not as skilled as Achilles, and he was slain by the Trojan Hector.

Tales From Troy (Continued)

Now Achilles needed new armor. Thetis went to Hephaestus, the blacksmith of the gods, and asked him to make for Achilles a magnificent helmet, sword, and shield. Achilles wore them when he rejoined the war the next day.

Vowing revenge for his friend's death, Achilles pursued Hector. Yet every time he approached the Trojan, Apollo sent a misty rain, so Achilles couldn't see him. The fighting continued, loud, confusing, and bloody, for a long time. At last, Achilles spied a Greek soldier leaning on Troy's city wall. The soldier was wearing Achilles' own armor, the helmet and shield that Patroklos had borrowed. Achilles realized that the soldier was no Greek; it was the Trojan Hector.

Watching from Mount Olympus, the gods and goddesses begged Zeus to intervene. "It is fate," Zeus reminded them, as they watched Achilles slay Hector on the battlefield. "It is fate."

The war continued, with Paris, a Trojan warrior, taking a more active role on the battlefield. He was a nervous soldier and a poor shot, but one day as he spied Achilles, he heard a voice in his ear.

"Shoot the arrow," Apollo whispered. "You'll be a hero when you strike him. Shoot!"

The arrow Paris shot wobbled from his bow, but Apollo steadied it and sent it skimming along the ground. Achilles suddenly felt a sharp pain in his left heel and was annoyed that he would have to leave the battle to have it bandaged. And why, he wondered, did the pain spread so quickly through his whole body? Why could he no longer move?

Meanwhile, Thetis flew over the battlefield, looking for her son. She had a terrible feeling that something had gone wrong. When Thetis saw Achilles' dead body with the arrow poking out of his heel, she quickly thought back to the day when she had dipped him in the River Styx — holding him by his left heel. His only remaining mortal part was where Paris struck and killed him.
She left the battlefield filled with terrible grief.

Odysseus and Ajax began to fight for Achilles' marvelous armor. Odysseus won, and the shame of losing caused Ajax to kill himself. But Thetis paid no attention. All she could think of was the centaur's long-ago prediction: *"The Greek army will need Achilles to capture Troy. He will be a hero, but he will die there."* Fate, again, had had the last word.

Homer's Heroes

To describe characters in *The Iliad* and *The Odyssey*, Homer relied on similes and metaphors. Both are types of comparisons. A simile uses the words *like* or *as* to compare one thing to another. A metaphor makes a comparison without using *like* or *as*. A simile says one thing is *like* another, and a metaphor says one thing *is* another.

In *The Iliad*, Stentor was a Greek soldier with a **harsh**, **loud voice**. But Homer used a metaphor and a simile to say this more effectively.

Homer described Stentor as "having a voice of *bronze*. His cry was *as loud as the cry of fifty men.*"

Read the description of each character below. On the line that follows, write a simile or metaphor to express the quality written in boldface type.

1. Cassandra, a Trojan princess and prophetess, was very **truthful**.

_____

_____

2. Odysseus, a leader of the Greek troops, was **intelligent**.

_____

_____

3. Ajax, a Greek warrior, was known for his **bravery**.

_____

_____

4. Patroklos, a Greek soldier and Achilles' best friend, was **loyal**.

_____

_____

5. Helen, Menelaus' wife and Queen of Sparta, was very **beautiful**.

_____

_____

6. Penthesilea, an Amazon queen who fought for Troy, **shot** her bow and arrow **very accurately**.

_____

_____

Make a Trojan Horse

After ten long years of fighting outside the walls of Troy, the Greeks were no closer to victory than they had been at the start of the war. Odysseus, captain of the Greek forces, had a new idea. Together with the builder Epeus, he created a giant wooden horse from the wood of their ships. Then they rolled the horse up to Troy's city gates. Greek soldiers were hidden inside.

As part of the plan, Sinon, another Greek soldier, let himself be captured. He told the Trojans that the horse was a sacrifice to Athena, and that anyone who had the horse would be protected by the goddess. "The Greeks have turned and gone home in defeat," Sinon lied. "This sacrifice was meant to carry them safety on the seas. But now that they have gone, it will keep you safe, as well."

Cassandra, the prophetess, cried, "Beware of Greeks bearing gifts," but no one listened to her. Apollo had given Cassandra the gift of prophecy, but also a curse. "When you speak," Apollo said, "no one will ever believe you."

King Priam brought the horse into the city and declared a victory celebration. Late that night, after the tired Trojans were asleep, Greek soldiers climbed out of their hiding place in the horse. They opened the gates to the rest of the Greek troops, who captured the city and won the war.

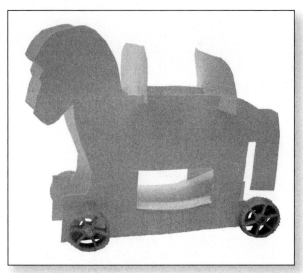

The Trojan Horse has become the symbol of the Trojan War. Just as the Greeks built their horse from the materials around them, you can use everyday craft supplies to make a horse that Athena would love!

Follow These Steps

1. Cut out the pieces for your Trojan Horse: two bodies, two yokes, and one base.

2. Carefully cut along the dotted lines on the bodies and yokes. Use a hole punch to make neat holes where indicated at the base of each horse.

3. Cut two 2¹/₂-inch lengths of your drinking straw. Discard the rest.

4. Your horse is nearly ready to decorate, but it's best to assemble it first to see what the final product will be. Assemble your horse by placing the two sides of the body in front of you. Slide one of the yokes into the front slits of each body piece.

Make a Trojan Horse (Continued)

5. Still holding the horse together, slide the base into the rectangular hole at the bottom of the horse. It should fit snugly.

6. Slide the second yoke into the back slits of the horse.

7. Slide each drinking straw through a set of holes. The straws are now the axles for the pasta wheels, so you can put your second set of wheels on the horse.

8. Squeeze one end of each straw piece and place it through the center of a pasta wheel. A small piece of straw will come through the hole.

9. Your horse is now complete. You can take it apart to paint or decorate it as it is. Be careful to keep the pasta wheels from becoming soaked with paint. Decorate creatively, thinking of what would most please Athena.

Hint
Use your god and goddess booklet to look up Athena's symbols. Can you represent one of them on your horse?

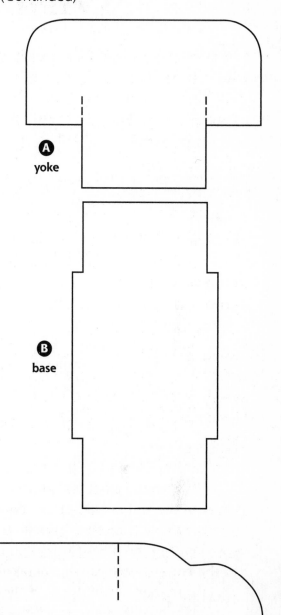

A yoke

B base

C horse

Cut out this rectangle.

On the Way to Ithaka

B lown off course by gusty winds, Odysseus' ship finally landed on the island of the Cyclops. Nearly starving and dying of thirst, Odysseus and his men saw with great relief the flocks of sheep and goats that grazed on the land. Now, at last, the sailors could eat, drink, and rest before setting off again for Ithaka.

Odysseus took 12 men with him to explore the island, leaving the rest to guard the ship. Odysseus soon discovered a cave filled with cheese and milk. As he and his men rejoiced over their discovery, the owner of the cave walked in.

The sight of the giant Cyclops silenced them. He was a one-eyed giant with the strength of many men. When he and his flocks were safely in the cave, he rolled a boulder in front of its entrance. Odysseus and his men were trapped.

"Greetings," said Odysseus. "In the name of Zeus, I have come to ask for your hospitality. My men and I are hungry and thirsty."

"No," roared the giant. "I am Polyphemus, the Cyclops. What do I care about the name of Zeus?" Suddenly reaching out a massive hand, he grabbed two sailors and ate them.

Odysseus and his companions watched fearfully as the giant fell asleep.

The next day Polyphemus ate four more sailors. Odysseus had a plan for escape, and it was now time to act. He emptied his wine flask into a bowl and offered it to the giant. The Cyclops drank it happily.

"Tell me your name," he roared. "You, who offer me this delicious potion. What do others call you?"

"I am Noman," replied Odysseus, offering the giant more wine.

When the giant fell asleep, Odysseus directed his men to sharpen one end of a wooden beam that held up the cave's ceiling. They charred one end of the beam in the fire. Suddenly they dashed at Polyphemus, puncturing his eye.

When the other Cyclops on the island heard Polyphemus's shouts of pain, they came to the entrance of his cave and asked him what was wrong.

"Noman has hurt me," Polyphemus cried, so the other Cyclops shrugged and left.

Then Polyphemus rolled the stone away from the cave's entrance. He began to feel around the floor of his cave, hoping to catch the men in his giant hand as they rushed to escape. But Odysseus directed his men to tie themselves to the underside of the giant's sheep, so all Polyphemus felt was his flock heading out to pasture.

When Odysseus and his men were safely on their ship again, Odysseus called back to the Cyclops. "Cyclops, you should know that it was Odysseus who punished you for refusing to show hospitality as the gods demand."

The giant roared a reply. "And you should know that my father is Poseidon, who will curse your seaward journey and keep you from your home as long as the gods will permit."

The Cyclops's curse was heard by Poseidon. And Odysseus' return trip from Troy lasted ten years, as long as the war itself.

Everyday Greek

Many modern expressions refer to characters and events that Homer described in *The Iliad* and *The Odyssey*.

Read through the list below. Each modern expression is written in boldface, followed by a sentence using the expression. Read these carefully. Use the context clues to help you understand the modern meaning of the expression, and write its modern meaning on the line. Then, use your knowledge, notes, and a reference book to recall the source of the expression. Write the source in the second line after the expression.

The first one has been done for you.

The Judgment of Paris Choosing between my two best friends is like making the judgment of Paris. Modern Meaning: *The Judgment of Paris means making a decision that's bound to leave someone upset.*

Mythological Reference: *The Judgment of Paris refers to Paris' choice of Aphrodite as the "fairest" goddess.*

1. Achilles' Heel I tried hard to cut down on sugar, but chocolate is my Achilles' heel.

Modern Meaning: _____

Mythological Reference: _____

2. "Beware of Greeks bearing gifts" When the rival team brought us a new soccer ball, the coach reminded us to "beware of Greeks bearing gifts."

Modern Meaning: _____

Mythological Reference: _____

3. Cassandra When I predicted rain on the day of the picnic, my classmates called me a Cassandra.

Modern Meaning: _____

Mythological Reference: _____

4. Odyssey In search of my book bag, I wandered from classroom to classroom. I made an odyssey throughout the school building.

Modern Meaning: _____

Mythological Reference: _____

5. Epic Proportions The story of the lost dog became a tale of epic proportions as he told it again and again.

Modern Meaning: _____

Mythological Reference: _____

Making Connections

Dionysus

This chapter offers closing activities and ideas to to celebrate the conclusion of your students' mythology unit. Each activity has either a "real life" or cross-curricular connection, including links to library/ research skills, physical education, and even cooking! Planning ahead, especially for Let's Have a Pantheon! (page 73) and Festival for Dionysus (page 74) will allow your students to work on their individual assignments throughout the unit.

Mythology in the Marketplace

Students may be surprised to discover the number of familiar products that bear mythological names.

MATERIALS

⚜ Mythology in the Marketplace reproducible (page 79) ⚜ dictionary of classical mythology or encyclopedia

HERE'S HOW

1. Ask students to list familiar products or brands that have Greek names. Students may be surprised to realize that Midas mufflers, Nike sneakers, and Ajax cleaning products are named for mythological characters.

2. Choose one example to discuss with the class (Ajax is done for you on the worksheet). With the class, identify the character and list his or her positive qualities. Explain that product manufacturers want consumers to associate only the character's positive qualities with the product.

3. With the class, write a brief statement that explains why you think the manufacturer chose this character to represent the product.

4. Students can complete the worksheet as a class, in small groups, or alone.

Let's Have a Pantheon!

As a concluding activity, have students present first-person oral reports on memorable characters in Greek mythology—whether ones they've read about in this book or on their own. Because information is plentiful and often contradictory, it's best to limit student research and writing. The following information is usually enough to generate a short oral report:

> Complete name (or names) of the character

> Character's family background

> Symbols associated with the character

> Special abilities or responsibilities of the character

> One episode from the character's life that illustrates his or her unique characteristics

Once students have gathered the necessary information, they can turn their research into a first-person oral report to be presented to the class. If students wish to dress up as their characters, the Dress Greek! activity (page 80) may be helpful.

The list of characters at right (some covered in this book, some not) may be helpful as you assign characters for this project.

Write an Encomium

For a simpler research-based project, you may wish to have your students write *encomia*, tributes to a mythological hero. In these tributes, which were recited aloud, ancient Greeks related the background, adventures, and admirable qualities of their heroes.

Assign each of your students a "memorable mortal" or Olympian god or goddess, and then have them write an encomium to recite to the class.

Olympian Gods and Goddesses

Aphrodite	Hephaestus
Apollo	Hera
Ares	Hermes
Artemis	Hestia
Athena	Poseidon
Demeter	Zeus
Hades (lives in underworld)	

Monsters/Mythical Creatures

Cerberus	Medusa
Chiron	Minotaur
Circe	Nemesis
Cyclops	Pegasus
The Furies	Sphynx

Memorable Mortals

Achilles	Medea
Agamemnon	Odysseus
Ajax	Paris
Andromeda	Penelope
Cassandra	Perseus
Helen of Troy	Priam
Jason	Theseus

Other Memorable Immortals

Atlas	Mother Earth
Cronos	The Muses
Daphne	The Nymphs
Echo	Pan
Helios	Pandora
Midas	

Interview a God or Goddess

Students can mimic their favorite talk show hosts or news personalities by interviewing gods, goddesses, and even monsters. As a class, brainstorm questions that interviewers ask, whether the who, what, where questions about a specific event, such as Heracles' labors, or the more general questions asked in a personality profile.

Pair students, assigning one the role of interviewer and the other the immortal role. They can outline their "Q and A," dress the part, and present their interviews to the class.

Festival for Dionysus

The ancient Greeks performed and watched a great deal of drama. In fact, the word *drama* means "to do" in Greek, just as the word *actor* means "to lead." Drama festivals, held in large amphitheaters, were dedicated to Dionysus, god of wine and fertility. The Athens festival known as the Dionysia lasted for five days every spring.

Playwrights wrote both tragedies and comedies. Tragedies often focused on mythological or heroic characters, while comedies centered on ordinary mortals. Actors and chorus members, who were all men, wore simple costumes—sometimes just regular clothing—and masks with oversize features so even the most distant audience members could see them.

The Dionysia, like a number of other festivals, was a playwrights' competition featuring three tragedies and three comedies. Laurel wreaths were awarded to the writers of the best comedy and best tragedy. Audience members were loud in their pleasure or displeasure. Actors sometimes resorted to bribing the audience with nuts for their silence and applause.

MATERIALS

§ a variety of myths that can be acted out

HERE'S HOW

Divide the class into groups of at least five students each. From the myths presented in this book, or others you have read as a class, assign one to each group. You may wish to allow the groups to choose their own.

Each group can divide (or you can assign) the roles, including a chorus to introduce and conclude the mini-play. Each student can perform as both a chorus member and another character if necessary.

Each group will need to develop lines, create a title, make masks (see Make a Mask, page 75), and rehearse their mini-play, so at least three class sessions will be needed. If students wish to dress as the ancient Greeks did, Dress Greek! (page 80) may be helpful.

When students are ready to perform, schedule several plays for the same day and award laurel wreaths (see tip on page 77) to each group of students.

Dress Greek!

Your students can easily create a Greek-style outfit from an old bed sheet, a length of fabric, or even old beach towels. (Students may want to choose the style they prefer, whether for adult male, young male, or female, before purchasing fabric.) Affluent Greeks wore jewelry and decorations; students can find examples at museum Web sites. Students can use such research to inspire the decoration of their own Greek clothing.

The most desirable fabric for clothes was Egyptian linen. Fabric was often dyed red, yellow, green, or purple. Many Greeks wore simple, one-piece cloaks as outerwear.

Grown men usually wore ankle-length *chitons*, or tunics. Boys, soldiers, and laborers wore their chitons to the knee. Women and girls wore ankle-length chitons or more elaborate tunics called peplos.

Students can follow the directions on the Dress Greek! reproducible (page 80) to make their own chitons.

Make a Mask

Actors and chorus members wore masks with exaggerated features and large mouth holes for speaking. Most students have probably seen the comedy and tragedy masks that are symbols of drama today. Your students will want to create several masks to portray the range of emotion—from surprise to sorrow—dictated by their characters.

For quick and easy animal masks, purchase animal-themed paper plates. Students can cut small holes for each eye, the nose, and the mouth. When the mask fits, students can punch holes on each side and thread yarn or string long enough to hold the mask in place.

MATERIALS

- heavy paper plates
- yarn or string
- hole punch
- paper scraps, glitter, and other decorative materials
- glue
- scissors

HERE'S HOW

1. Taking turns with a partner, each student holds a paper plate to his or her face and asks the partner to sketch the position of eyes, nose, and mouth.

2. Students can cut out a hole for eyes, nose, and mouth according to the expression of the mask. The rounded top and bottom of the plate can also be shaped. The entire mask can then be decorated. When the mask is complete, students can use a hole punch to create holes on either side (near the ears). They can then thread yarn or string through each hole to hold the mask in place.

Each student may need more than one mask.

Greek Games: The Olympics

The Olympic Games, which date from 776 BC, were held every four years in Olympia as part of a festival for Zeus. Wars were halted so athletes and spectators—sometimes as many as 50,000—could travel safely to Olympia. There, visitors found a compound of buildings that included temples, stadiums, a hotel, a building where the Olympic Council met, and even a training ground.

On the first day of the games, the athletes, all men (who competed nude!), visited the temple of Zeus. They each swore an oath that they had trained for ten months and would follow the rules of the games. Then the events began!

A herald announced the winner after each event, but prizes were awarded only on the last day of the games. Winners' prizes were modest: laurel wreaths to wear on their heads. The prestige and honor each winner brought to his hometown was the real reward—along with the money and gold many towns gave to their winners.

Ask your students to compare modern Olympic games with those of ancient times. The list below of ancient events is a good place to start.

Ancient Events

Pentathlon: This five-sport contest was designed to find the very best athlete of the games. It included discus throwing, javelin throwing, running, jumping, and wrestling.

Running: The running events included three main races: the stade (1 length of the track), the diaulos (2 lengths of the track), and the dolichos (24 lengths of the track). The track was about 640 feet long.

Running in armor: Runners sprinted while wearing a shield and carrying a metal helmet.

Horse racing: Horse races were very dangerous for the riders, who rode bareback and sometimes dismounted to run alongside their horses.

Chariot racing: Also risky, chariot racing involved either two or four horses pulling a chariot for 12 laps of the track. Drivers risked collision with other chariots, as up to 40 raced at once.

Wrestling and boxing: The wrestling events included upright wrestling, ground wrestling, and pankration, a combination of wrestling and boxing that allowed any maneuver no matter how dangerous.

A Classroom Olympics

For a great Greek celebration, design a modern Olympics based loosely on the ancient Games. Divide the class into at least four teams, instructing each to choose a mythological name and mascot. Teams, wearing color-coded T-shirts, can rotate through the following outdoor events (or add your own). Award laurel wreaths (see box right) to the winning team for each event. You may want to begin your Olympics with athletes pledging to follow the rules, just as the ancient athletes did!

Modern Events

◇ For chariot racing, substitute a three-legged race, in which partners run a short distance with one leg each tied together with a bandana or piece of fabric.

> For horse racing, substitute a wheelbarrow race, where partners take turns holding one another's feet while the "horse" runs on his or her hands.

> For foot races, substitute sack races, both individual and team relay.

◇ For running in armor, substitute the water run, where team members relay race carrying a full cup of water. The winner is the fastest team with the most water remaining.

> For javelin throwing, substitute an egg toss, where partners toss an uncooked egg to one another trying to catch it in a spoon, moving further apart for each round. Teams are eliminated as their eggs fall and break.

◇ For discus throwing, substitute a beanbag toss at a cardboard cutout of a Cyclops. Points are awarded for tossing the beanbag though the Cyclops' eye hole.

To Make a Laurel Wreath

*F*or each student in the class, cut a long, leafy branch from a laurel, forsythia, or azalea bush that needs pruning. If the branches are too stiff to bend, place the cut ends in water overnight. Then bend the branches into a circle and tie with fishing line or wire.

A Greek Feast

These two simple recipes can involve the whole class in chopping, stirring, and tasting! Spanakopita is a Greek dish traditionally made with filo dough. Simple Spanakopitakia (little spanakopita) calls for refrigerated roll dough instead. Easy Ambrosia, the food of the gods, is a simple dessert recipe that doesn't involve any cooking.

Kali Orexi (Good Eating)!

Simple Spanakopitakia

2 tablespoons olive oil

2 medium onions, chopped

2 10-ounce packages frozen, chopped spinach, thawed and drained

$^1/_2$ cup dill, chopped

$^1/_4$ cup parsley, chopped

1 tablespoon lemon juice

1 6-ounce package of feta, crumbled

4 packages of refrigerated, ready-to-bake crescent rolls (8 rolls per pack)

1. Heat oil in large pan and saute onion until wilted. Add spinach, dill, parsley, and lemon juice. Stir well. Remove mixture from heat. Stir in feta cheese.

2. On nonstick cookie sheets, unroll and separate the crescent rolls. The rolls will look like big triangles. Spoon one heaping tablespoonful onto the fat end of each triangle. Fold in each roll's corners, wrapping the long end around the spinach mixture. (Some spinach mixture may be visible; this is fine.)

3. Bake the spanakopitakia in a preheated 350° oven for 10–12 minutes, or until golden brown. Eat while warm.

Yield: 32 pieces

Easy Ambrosia

1 8-ounce container frozen whipped topping, softened

2 $^1/_2$ cups coconut, shredded

$^1/_2$ cup walnuts, chopped

1 8-ounce can fruit cocktail, drained well

1 8-ounce can pineapple chunks, drained well

1 11-ounce can mandarin oranges, drained well

3 cups miniature marshmallows

1 teaspoon ground cinnamon

In a large bowl, mix all ingredients well. Chill for 30 minutes.

Yield: 10 servings

To round out your Greek feast, consider serving some of the following simple, prepared foods:

◇ olives

◇ grapes

◇ pita bread

◇ hummus

◇ fruit nectars or juices

◇ green salad

Mythology in the Marketplace

Many modern products are named for characters and places in Greek mythology. This is no accident; manufacturers choose names carefully for their products, hoping that consumers will associate the positive qualities of the character with the product.

Several familiar products with mythological names are listed below. For each product, identify the character or place it refers to by consulting your notes, an encyclopedia, or a dictionary of classical mythology. List the positive attributes of the character or place. Then explain briefly why a manufacturer might choose that name for a product. The first one is done for you.

Brand Name and Product	Character	Positive Qualities	Explanation
Ajax (cleaning products)	Ajax, a hero of the Trojan War	strong, brave, very powerful	This soap's cleaning power is as strong as Ajax.
Atlas Van Lines (movers)			
Amazon.com (booksellers and more)			
Olympus (cameras)			
Nike athletic (athletic wear)			
Hermès (leather goods)			

Name _____   Date _____

Dress Greek!

Make a chiton (tunic) to dress like a citizen of ancient Greece. They wore clothes of many colors, so using leftover fabric is ideal. Bed sheets or towels will also work. The Greeks wore jewelry, accessories, and hair ornaments, so be creative as you "dress Greek"!

MATERIALS

> fabric, a bed sheet, or two towels
> 2 or 4 large safety pins
> belt or piece of rope
> decorative materials

FOLLOW THESE INSTRUCTIONS

Tip: Women, girls, and older men wore chitons that fell to the ankle. Boys, laborers, and soldiers wore chitons that fell to the knee.

1. Measure a length of fabric (you can also use a sheet or a towel) from the forehead to your knees or ankles. The fabric should be wide enough to reach around your body comfortably. (Hint: Measure while wearing clothes similar to those you'll be wearing for the performance.)

2. Sew or staple one side of the fabric or sheet. If using two towels, sew both sides. You now have a long tube. Turn it right-side up and slip it on. Pull the top edge up to just below the armpits.

3. Use pins to secure the chiton.

   • For a female's chiton, use two sets of large safety pins (or brooches) to connect the front and the back of the chiton across the shoulders. One set of pins connects the chiton close to the neck. The second set of pins should connect the chiton across the shoulders.

   • For a male's chiton, use two large safety pins to connect the front and the back of the chiton across the shoulders. This will create a draped effect across the front and shoulders.

4. Tie a length of rope or a belt around the waist if desired. (Women and girls sometimes wore their chitons loose.) Decorate the chiton as desired.